A Zany Slice of Tuscany

La Bella Figura and Other Italian Concepts That Elude Me

Ivanka Di Felice

A Zany Slice of Tuscany
Copyright © 2016 Ivanka Di Felice
All rights reserved.

All images are copyrighted and not to be used without permission.

Cover design by Joe Shepherd
Edited by P. N. Waldygo at DesertSageBookEditor.com
Formatting by Polgarus Studio

The story you are about to read is true, though some names have been changed to protect the innocent, namely the author.

ISBN-13: 9781983296475

Also by Ivanka Di Felice:

A Zany Slice of Italy (Book 1 of the Italian Living Series)
Zany Renovations in Tuscany (Book 3 of the Italian Living Series)
My Zany Life: Growing Up in a Rooming House

A restored villa in the Val di Chio

For Tata

"Anticipation is the greatest part of any venture."
—Leah Pakosh

Contents

Preface 1
Chapter 1 Roman "Holiday" 2
Chapter 2 Italy Calls, We Answer 6
Chapter 3 Touring Tata 9
Chapter 4 "If You've Seen One, You've Seen Them All" 18
Chapter 5 Mischievous *Bella* Italia 22
Chapter 6 Tata "Sees" Florence 26
Chapter 7 Back to School 30
Chapter 8 Italian History—Like It or Not 35
Chapter 9 Roundabout Ruckus 42
Chapter 10 Home Invasion 46
Chapter 11 Rustic Times Call for Rustic Measures 49
Chapter 12 "Mother Sitting" 56
Chapter 13 Tuscany, according to "the Experts" 62
Chapter 14 The "Hardly Noticeable" Guestapos 65
Chapter 15 Captivating Castle 67
Chapter 16 Glen and the Seven Slaves 71
Chapter 17 The Old and the Restless 75
Chapter 18 Earnest Ernesta 81
Chapter 19 Olive, Our Love 86
Chapter 20 Four Saps in a Tub 93
Chapter 21 Coming to a "Grinding" Halt 103
Chapter 22 Auto Lotto 107
Chapter 23 Rom-antic 110
Chapter 24 The Big Wig 115
Chapter 25 Doctor Dear 119
Chapter 26 Homeless Bound 122

Chapter 27	Large Black Capital P	125
Chapter 28	Cinque Terre-rist	128
Chapter 29	Chick Magnet	135
Chapter 30	*Bello* Marcello and "the Albanian"	139
Chapter 31	Speeding with Seniors	143
Chapter 32	To Be or Not to Be . . .	148
Chapter 33	Lamb-asted	151
Chapter 34	Table Nazi	156
Chapter 35	We "Chianti" Find a House!	160
Chapter 36	Arrivederci	164
Chapter 37	A Day in Florence	169
Chapter 38	See You Later, Navigator	172
Chapter 39	The Color Gods Must Be Crazy	174
Chapter 40	Cultivating Saintly Qualities	177
Chapter 41	The Amalfi Coast	181
Chapter 42	Walk the Path of the Gods, Drive Home with the Devil	186
Chapter 43	Surprise in the Oven	189
Chapter 44	Enchanting Journeys	193
Chapter 45	"See Naples and Die"	198
Chapter 46	Living *La Dolce Vita*—Anywhere!	202
Acknowledgments		209

Preface

First, let me assure you that we are not on Canada's Most Wanted list, and we can return at any time. We have chosen a life in Italy because the pros far outweigh the cons. Italy is legendary for its fabulous food and wine, glorious scenery and art. To boot, the people are generous, hospitable, hardworking, and, let's admit, beautiful. I always say that "Italy has it all, and if you have never visited, you should."

I write humor and thus have chosen to write about the quirky situations that we encounter here, simply because they are funny.

So please read my book with a sense of humor and know that I wrote it with one.

Chapter 1

Roman "Holiday"

I recall my first trip to Rome with my husband, David. Though my Italian love affair began long before I met him . . .

I fell in love with Italy the minute I spotted that peach-colored swing coat in Florence more than twenty years ago. Though it was ruinously expensive, I had to possess it. Being nineteen at the time certainly helped me decide. I handed over my MasterCard, put on the coat, and pranced out onto the beckoning cobblestone streets of Florence.

From that moment on, I was enchanted with a country that could produce such an exquisite item.

My next inevitable step was to marry an Italian, for Italians, too, possessed an enchanting air. They were dark, handsome, and stylish beyond any North American's dreams.

Then, once married to an Italian, I assumed my days would suddenly become leisurely and carefree, my hair would grow long and thick, and my bust size would miraculously increase. I would take to wearing frilly white linen skirts, designed by Dolce and Gabbana. At last, I could sport ridiculously large black sunglasses without anyone assuming I was hiding from the law, and my lips would take on a permanent *Italian Vogue* pout.

For ages, I'd envisioned strolling down quaint alleys, sipping fine Tuscan wine in a piazza, and discussing art and history with the nobles, as we visited a vast array of galleries. In my dreams, passionate opera music always played in the background. My husband, meanwhile, dreamed of fast cars racing down Italian motorways.

And so, after our years of fantasizing, my prince agreed to take his *principessa* to the land his forefathers had built.

I waved "*Ciao*" to the throngs of jealous coworkers at my stressful brokerage job, and we embarked on a two-week holiday.

Moments after landing in Rome, our "adventure" indeed began.

At this point I must warn you: Italian princes always come with relatives, my prince being no exception. So instead of the elegant chauffeur with the dark limo I'd dreamed about, *Zio* ("uncle") is our designated driver and has been anxiously awaiting our arrival.

"*Ciao, Zio,*" we greet him, with the customary double kiss. "How are you?"

But he has no time to reply or inquire about our trip, because "pleasantries" consist of *Zio* carrying on in colorful language about how "those dirty rotten scoundrels make you pay for parking wherever you go!" Naturally, *Zio* would never take part in *any* crazy government scheme to collect taxes; hence, he scurries us off to his illegally parked car.

Yet he does have time to add, "Lunch is ready, we must hurry."

Our "holiday" continues as we pull onto the highway, and *Zio* proves you can be almost eighty and still cherish the dream of one day becoming a racecar driver. Speed limits are mere suggestions—apparently ridiculous ones, at that. He also confirms his deep affinity for the passing lane and leaves it only when drivers more maniacal than he is suddenly flash their lights, signaling him to get out of the way. I look at my prince and sigh, for somehow I doubt that his dreams of fast cars on Italian motorways involved an elderly uncle driving out of control.

A small "yelp" escapes me, and *Zio* finally notices that I am terrified, even though I have been frightened from the moment he peeled out of the parking lot.

He glances back and assures me, "I am a very safe driver," then elaborates, "The few accidents I've had were not really my fault."

I look out the window to distract myself, but all that my eye catches are the many colorful roadside bouquets, in honor of people who died on these very spots. I comfort myself with the pleasant thought that death will be instantaneous.

I further console myself by thinking that we should arrive soon, thanks to *Zio*'s driving like an escaped lunatic and because my husband had said his uncle "lives in Rome." I'd imagined a grand villa in the heart of the city, surrounded by glorious monuments. Yet as *Zio* keeps driving, farther and farther into the ugly graffiti-marked suburbs, I soon discover that "lives in Rome" is a relative expression—a secret I will keep from my envious coworkers. I can at least say he lives "off the beaten track," though only now do I realize that is not always a good thing.

Believing in miracles at this point, we arrive at *Zio*'s cement compound, and within seconds, he rushes us in to eat. "The Slow Movement," Italy's famous slogan, does not appear to be a concept *Zio* has in any way embraced. Rather, his motto is clearly "Time is of the essence"—but perhaps at his age, it really is.

Inside, we find a large extended family waiting for us to feast with them.

Each course is accompanied by a commentary on how Italian food is the most delicious in the world, with David and I knowing full well that no one in the room has ever tried any other type of cuisine. They would most likely choose death over dining in a foreign restaurant.

Zia ("aunt") has made enough food for fifty people and is determined that we finish all of it.

"C'mon, you must eat more!" she implores and heaps more food onto my plate, despite my protests.

The conversation revolves mainly around the superiority of all things Italian. The TV is on full blast, so everyone has to yell. My nerves are still fragile from the drive, and I find all of the shouting quite unsettling. I would like to dispel the myth that Italian families merely *sound* as if they are always fighting. After a few hours, I realize that they actually *are* fighting a good portion of the time. Yet since matters of consequence are involved, such as what brand of pasta is best, it is understandable that heated arguments would ensue.

"Do you like my wine?" *Zio* asks. I manage to nod and keep a straight face, as he launches into a long-winded tribute to the vile liquid. I assure you that mere mortals, or their livers, could not have lived to tell this tale. But at least my aspiration of drinking "wine" in Italy has been fulfilled.

The opera music of my dreams is now replaced by loud accordion music that will not end. I believe *Zio*'s strong wine will come in handy after all.

After lunch, *Zio* offers to give us a tour. I am pleased, because I assume he means of Rome. But I am mistaken. *Zio* means doing the circuit of his prized vegetable garden. I soon learn that it really is possible to deliver an entire one-hour sermon on how to grow tomatoes. As a bonus, he shows us the vast compound he has built for himself and his children and throws in a mini thesis on the virtues of cement.

Zia also has some excursions in mind. Hers, though, involve more erratic driving through the neighborhood, visiting cousins who were not able to make it for lunch today—nor did my Italian prince even know they existed.

And so we "tour" "Rome." We see Amerigo and Gino and Mario and Anna and Rosa and her children and their children and everyone else's children, and when nearly every one of them asks me, "Isn't Rome beautiful?" I almost weep as I reply, "I've heard it so said."

Some days "touring" is easier than others; we just need to go up some steps for lunch, down a few steps for dinner, and across the hall for dessert. Had I only known our "holiday" would involve so little walking, I certainly would have packed a pair of high heels.

Two weeks pass and I survive more relatives, more superior Italian food, and four people simultaneously speaking to me in a language I can barely understand.

I try to look on the bright side: after our Roman "holiday," it is with great relief that I return to my hectic brokerage job for a slower pace of life. At least, no one is jealous of me anymore.

And, at long last, my husband has stopped dreaming about fast cars on Italian motorways.

Regardless, this visit left its mark on us, especially for two months afterward as we tried to lose the excess weight. But the seed was planted, and we knew we would eventually return. Italy was beckoning, and one day we would answer her call.

Chapter 2

Italy Calls, We Answer

It's been years since that initial visit, and a lot has happened. We answered Italy's call and moved here. *Zio* is still alive and continues to drive like an escaped lunatic. I am that much wiser, thus, when we visit *Zio* "in Rome," I willingly hop onto the overcrowded, smelly bus in the stagnant summer heat. *Zia*, in her eighties, still cooks as if she's catering a wedding feast and is no less intent that we finish it all off.

Regardless, we will never forget their hospitality and continue to visit them. Sometimes when we are in "Rome," we even get to see a sight or two.

Yet our hearts belong to Tuscany. The old farmhouse we live in has grown to be home. I now scoff at décor magazines depicting perfectly matched furniture and uniform floors. I have come a long way from the woman I was when we first rented this house. I'd almost wept when the "new" (in Tuscan time, twenty years is not considered old) dishwasher was delivered. The color was off by a few shades and didn't match the ancient stove. The locals looked at me as if I were crazy, when, teary-eyed, I pointed out the four-shade difference.

Yet I have grown and have created a new version of "mix and match." Bachelors around the world would be quick to patent our floor, because the speckled granite refuses to reveal whether it is freshly washed or not, and don't ever drop a coin on it—you will never find it.

Our guests continue to enjoy privileged views of glorious sunsets—albeit only from their bathroom window—as the hilltop town of Castiglion Fiorentino sparkles in the distance.

The old farmhouse we call home

Our two hens, Roberta and Barbara, happily scavenge in the fields, unless David is outside. Then they shadow him, never straying more than a few inches away. He spends more time with them than with me some days.

Each season brings with it a host of small pleasures and seasonal specialties, and I now participate in "fascinating" conversations revolving around fava beans that can be maintained for hours.

Spring brings warm weather and the comfort of a living room, for not every room in this house is "all season." Damp winters confine us to the kitchen, sitting in two lawn chairs next to the wood stove. Regardless, a deep contentment resides in us; material things do not bring true pleasure in life. I chant this mantra when my subscription to *Canadian House and Home* magazine arrives.

Summer brings an abundance of fresh vegetables from our garden and also brings my mother-in-law. I accept, and even smile, when she turns our house into a canning factory, with tomatoes balanced atop each of my elegant glass candleholders. Aside from my intrepid elderly mother-in-law who comes to work, no one else dares to vacation here during the scorching heat of summer.

As summer draws to a close, the chaotic, relentless visits from fun-loving *paesani* and relatives, including those from abroad, begin anew.

Chapter 3

Touring Tata

My father, Tata, as we call him, along with other relatives and certain guests, ensures that my original, albeit rather romanticized, notion of the life I will lead in Italy—and dream of, on rare occasions—will elude me. Tata is quite the character, and thinking of him puts a smile on my face. He lives in a high-end Toronto neighborhood and spends his time trapping raccoons in his backyard, then releasing them at the Home Depot parking lot a short distance away. A Jamaican tenant assists him and completes Tata's unlikely entourage. They have caught twenty-three critters in the last two months, fifty-six in total for the season. Meanwhile, Home Depot employees wonder where this scourge of raccoons in broad daylight is coming from.

Now that hunting season is over, though, it's time for Tata to head to Italy. We are looking forward to his visit. His antics always have us in stitches, because I know he says most of what he does for shock value. I'm grateful he has a sense of humor and that he's still able to travel at his age. Regardless, I'll let you judge whether the glamorous hilltop town of Cortona is ready for the likes of us.

Several times I offer to pick him up from the train station in Rome, but he adamantly refuses.

"Am I a baby? Then stop worrying about me," Tata says, perturbed by my insistence.

"Okay, fine. Get a pen, and I will give you directions." This is where I foolishly assume he is getting a pen and writing down this crucial information, rather than relying on his eighty-year-old memory.

He arrives in Rome exhausted. He looks for a taxi, because he cannot bother to recall the instructions I gave him.

"It will be three hundred euros to Castiglion Fiorentino," the taxi driver says.

The painful thought of digging deep into his pockets suddenly revives Tata's memory: *something about a train to Firenze* . . . Darn, he can't quite remember, but he refuses to participate in this rip-off scam involving taxis. Suddenly, he wishes he had bothered with that pen and paper.

I try not to worry but cannot help myself. Worse still, I realize that two trains are leaving the station for Florence within minutes of each other. One goes directly to Florence, while the other makes several stops en route, the latter being the one my father needs to take. I imagine my father, who lacks the patience of Job, taking the first train he comes across that says "Florence."

I phone him. "Hi, I wanted to make sure you're on the right train. There are two trains going to Florence. Make sure you are on the *regional* train."

Patently annoyed, he says, "I'm on the one that says Florence. See you soon," and hangs up.

I call him back, fearful. "But are you on the regional train?"

"I don't know," he says.

"Well, ask the guy next to you," I say.

I wait a minute, hear some garbled speech, and then my father says, "He doesn't know either." This lack of knowledge on the part of his fellow passenger annoys my father to no end.

There is a fifty-fifty chance he is on the right train.

The train slowly rolls out of the Rome station, while my father no doubt mentally urges the train conductor to speed it up.

He sits restlessly as the train makes stop after stop. After all, my dad's motto, like *Zio*'s, is, "Time is of the essence."

After what seems like an eternity, the train pulls into Castiglione del Lago. He lugs his suitcase down with great difficulty and impatiently looks for us. We are not there. He is appalled. Suddenly, his eighty-year-old memory kicks in—this is Castiglione *del Lago*, and we live in Castiglion *Fiorentino*. He is furious at having got off at the wrong stop—at whom I'm not sure, but I'm quite certain not with himself. In a panic, he asks a guy near the door to help him and his suitcase back onto the train. The man drags both of them up just as the train departs.

A half hour later, he arrives in Castiglion Fiorentino and finds us waiting for him on the platform. We greet him with double kisses, grateful he has made it.

We drive past the charming medieval town of Castiglion Fiorentino, situated on a hill between Arezzo and Cortona. In the distance rises the imposing tower Torre del Cassero, a symbol of past power and prestige during the fourteenth century. We continue through the panoramic Tuscan hillside of the Val di Chio, or Val di Dio ("Valley of God"), as referred to by locals. Surrounded by mountains and the hills where Castiglion Fiorentino is situated, it was once an important link between the Tyrrhenian Sea and the Adriatic Sea. Ruins of seven ancient castles, churches, monasteries, and little villages testify to this important past history. The valley is lush and fertile. The green-forested hills are interspersed with terraces of olive groves, country houses, and picturesque villages.

Val di Chio

We arrive at the stately stone farmhouse with green shutters that we're renting. Its vast grounds feature views of the hilltop town of Castiglion

Fiorentino in the background. A profusion of lavender borders the stone walkways around the house. We started with a few humble plants, and, after pruning last fall, we simply put the trimmed tops into the ground and this spring were rewarded for our simple effort. Large rosemary bushes scent the air. Everything grows so easily here. It's dead quiet, except for the sound of squawking pheasants in the surrounding fields. My father finally smiles.

"This is paradise," he says, as he looks around and gives his stamp of approval. "If I win the lottery, I'll buy this place for you. You can turn it into several rental apartments and earn lots of money."

We struggled here the first few years, as we tried odd jobs that tested our humility and patience, but we finally came to accept that work is scarce in Italy, and although we appear (in our own opinion) still young, in the realm of the Italian workforce we are not. Thus, when necessity demands, we go back to Canada to work, where we are not considered old but experienced. David does renovations, while I return to my brokerage firm, much to the astonishment of our Italian friends.

Because we have such opportunities, we can never actually claim to "live like a local." The stock market has also taken mercy on us, as has Eric, who employs us during the summer to look after his two vacation homes. By living an unpretentious life, such as drinking *vino sfuso* (usually, wine that did not make it to the oak barrels and is not considered worthy of bottling, commonly sold as house wine at local trattorias), instead of the finer Brunello, we are able to stay here and to stay sane. The children we used to teach are safer that way, too.

Since my dad has already begun planning the elaborate renovations, I don't have the heart to tell him that David and I are happy with things the way they are. We prefer our privacy and simple way of life, rather than slaving over tourists all day to make more money, which we then wouldn't have time to spend.

Besides, this estate has been in our landlord's family for more than 150 years, along with many other similar properties. The thought of selling even one of them would be out of the question. Thus, while sitting on millions in real estate, our landlady drives a beat-up purple car and complains about how little money they have. I suspect that her children will simultaneously sign the death certificate and the real estate contracts. Soon thereafter, they will drive up to their own restored villas in their newly purchased Ferraris. But our landlady is of the generation that wants to pass on a legacy to their children, parents who sacrifice everything for their offspring.

I laugh to myself and let my father dream. Hopefully, it will keep him occupied while he is here.

David carries in Tata's suitcase. A small quantity of clothes surrounds a large mosquito zapper he has brought us. Another "gift" is a gray plaid baseball cap with a Coors Light logo for David. A bonus feature is a beer opener under the peak. I muster up all of the enthusiasm I can to thank him, but David seems genuinely grateful. I envision our "elegant" dinner parties in the Tuscan countryside with David sporting his new hat, opening beers to the sound of mosquitoes being executed.

Tata and David, each sporting a baseball cap equipped with a beer opener under the peak

Along with a few clothing items, the mosquito executioner, and a large package of oatmeal, he has also packed his unfortunately indestructible Chinese flip-flops—the only "made in China" item that is durable. They were black but are currently speckled with various shades of paint from recent projects, broadcasting my father's deep love of primary colors.

The next morning at 7 a.m., there is a noise in the kitchen. It is Tata, and that means I will have to get up to make him breakfast.

He hovers over me, providing specific instructions on how he likes his well-traveled oatmeal. I stir the oatmeal with a large wooden spoon until it is done, according to his exacting standards. I leave it on the stove, while I gather a bowl and some utensils. But there is no need. He places the pot directly on the table, eliminating the need for cutlery by eating straight out of the pot with the wooden spoon.

Tata swears, "It tastes much better this way."

Perhaps this is a secret that Jamie Oliver is not aware of or is simply unwilling to share with the masses.

After breakfast, I do the dishes, while Tata takes a nap.

When he wakes up, I offer to take him to Siena.

He is keen on going. "Sure! While I'm here, I might as well see everything."

My father, always in a rush, is in a terrible hurry to get to Siena and utters his famous words "I'll be waiting in the car." This time, his words prove ludicrous because he is not the driver.

I hurry to get ready, while Tata impatiently sits in the car. Although the rest of Italy lives it, the Slow Movement seems to elude me—ironically, when I spend time with relatives in their eighties. I recall my mom's words: "Perhaps you are not living your dream but rather the one that mischievous *bella* Italia had up her sleeve for you. A dream that demands a full range of emotions daily." Knowing how happy we are, despite life not always delivering what I wanted, my mom added, "This shows that our dreams are not always the best for us."

I smile, as I approach Tata sitting in the car.

I get in and turn the key in the ignition. Startled, my dad looks out the window, expecting to see a fighter jet flying low over us.

"We have a slight problem with the car," I say. "But don't worry, it just *sounds* like we're about to take off."

As I pull out, Tata seems unnerved and holds onto the handle above with both hands.

I take the longer but more scenic route, so that my father can behold the lovely Tuscan countryside, with the golden earth glowing in the gorgeous landscape. We drive past many long-abandoned Leopoldine-style villas. I imagine the lives once lived in these enormous homes, currently in a state of near ruin, scattered among the vast fields.

Though I've driven this route several times, the beauty never ceases to amaze me. My father, though, has barely glanced out the window. Yet he is intent on knowing where we are and has his eyes firmly focused on the map in his lap. I point out a field of sunflowers in all of its splendor, but my father has found where we are on the map and will not be taking his eyes off that spot.

Field of sunflowers

I park in Sinalunga, and from there we take the train to Siena. After my last driving mishap in Siena, I don't want to take any chances. I was stuck at a red light on a steep hill, when the light turned green. I panicked, peeled out, and burned rubber, in a car that already sounded as if it was about to self-combust. I left a crowd of astonished locals and tourists in my wake. Hence, I think it's best we make our entrance by train this time.

I believe my father is happy, too. He looks up from his map and beams as he sees the station.

A small train, toylike, appears on the track. We hop into one of the three cars, and as we travel through the dramatic countryside of Siena, its wavy terrain scattered with farms and noble vineyards, my father returns to scrutinizing his map.

We arrive just in time for the noon sun to beat down mercilessly on us. My father and I trudge slowly through the crowded, narrow streets of Siena, making our way to Piazza del Campo, the main square of the historic center. My father is clearly annoyed that we aren't the only ones visiting Siena and curses the masses of tourists happily taking pictures. They are oblivious to my father's resolve to arrive at Piazza del Campo in record time for a man his age.

The problem with my father being eighty is that it happened virtually overnight. He went from being sixty-like to an eighty-year-old man, with all of the aches and difficulty in walking. Prior to that, he had been the epitome of health. So this age thing would take some getting used to.

With him cursing every interference, we arrive at the grand piazza. Regarded as one of Europe's greatest medieval squares, it is renowned worldwide for its beauty and architectural integrity. In fact, my father is no longer studying his map but is now examining menus displayed in the charming cafés in the square. Bent over, both hands behind his back, he squints, his head almost touching each menu.

"What the heck?" he says and then continues in even more colorful language. He has been able to decipher the prices, and his displeasure is evident to all onlookers. He is intent on finding a place to sit down that serves beer at a reasonable price: two things that do not go hand in hand in one of the most famous piazzas in the world. Nonetheless, I let him go ahead, from bar to bar, scrutinizing their menus, and wait for his subsequent outburst. I offer to pick up the tab, but he refuses to let either of us pay, "out of principle."

I lag behind until he yells, "Ivanka, we are leaving!"

We walk out of Piazza del Campo, with my dad never having glanced up at the grandeur and splendor of the public square. He leaves deeply disappointed with Siena.

Yet all is not lost. At the train station, beer is reasonably priced, so we grab a couple of beers from the self-serve fridge, pay the few euros, and sit down at a table facing the train tracks. My dad is happy at last, as he drinks cheap beer overlooking the greasy, junk-laden tracks. Perhaps he will have fond memories of Siena after all. I smile in recognition that one can be just as happy or even more so, judging by the look on my dad's face, sitting by train tracks as in an elaborate piazza. I realize that even those with little means (or with lots of money but with "principles") can enjoy small pleasures, whatever their surroundings. Better not tell that to the Italian Minister of Tourism.

I forgo the scenic route home and arrive in half the time it took us to get there.

David asks, "How did you like Siena?"

As my dad launches into his rant, I give him credit. He is the only person I know who can have a strong opinion about disliking a place that he has never really seen, though he has actually visited it. Few can make that claim.

David has picked a basket of sweet corn from his garden. He eagerly peels away the husks and discovers that his prized corn can be marketed as "calorie reduced," because only every third kernel has grown. Tata is nonetheless impressed with David's farming abilities.

I hurry to make dinner, *pici* (a thick, hand-rolled pasta, like a fat spaghetti, that originated in Siena) with a homemade *ragù* sauce to be served with calorie-reduced corn, while Tata takes a nap. After dinner, I clean up the mound of dishes, while the men play chess.

When I show signs of fatigue, Tata says, "You sure get tired easily."

I laugh. "I have jet lag from trying to keep up with you."

Chapter 4

"If You've Seen One, You've Seen Them All"

Day Two—7 a.m. In a sleepy stupor, I make my dad's breakfast. Still not trusting me, my dad stands over me and provides play-by-play instructions on how to prepare his oatmeal. He is very fussy about the process and explains the finer points, as he eats it out of the pot with a large wooden spoon.

"Today I would like to . . . ," begins my dad.

I fear his next words but relax when I realize his request involves driving all of five minutes.

". . . go to the supermarket to buy beer," he finishes.

At least, he will pay rapt attention to his surroundings. And so it would be. He has a grand old time examining and comparing beer prices at the supermarket and is truly ecstatic to come back with such great "souvenirs" from Italy and Germany.

The rest of the day is spent walloping my husband at chess. My father is really enjoying "Italy"—cheap beer and a son-in-law he can beat at chess with his eyes closed.

The phone rings. It is Anna and Francesco, inviting us for dessert. My father met them while they were visiting Canada and drove them to downtown Toronto. I asked them how they'd survived the drive, but they seemed confused, saying, "He is one of the calmest, most patient drivers we have ever had."

I nearly burst out laughing but caught myself just in time.

They are from Naples, and I have driven with Francesco, so everything is relative. Meanwhile, my sister, who had recently undergone foot surgery and was still on crutches, decided that hobbling through a crowded streetcar in rush hour was easier than enduring a drive with my father. But then, she is not married to a man from Naples.

I ask my father if he would like to see Arezzo on our way to Anna and Francesco's, and he says "Sure, why not, while I am here?"

I prepare a picnic for us to enjoy in the park in Arezzo. The views are quite stunning: classic Tuscan hillsides covered in olive groves and Cypress trees surrounding grand villas. Maybe my father will even smile in one of the pictures.

We arrive at the parking lot outside the city walls. Surprisingly, considering that Arezzo may have been one of the twelve most important Etruscan cities, there is an escalator that takes you up into the ancient historic center. David and I exit the car, while my father hesitates.

"Are you coming?" I ask.

"Are we in Arezzo?" he asks.

"Yes," I say. "We're going to have a picnic in the park and then look around."

He looks up at the ancient walls and asks, "Is it just another old town?"

"We're in Italy!" I say, laughing. "They are *all* old towns."

"Well, then, no need to bother," he says. "We don't have to see it."

"But we're already here. There's an escalator, so you don't have to walk, and I've packed a picnic for us—"

"We can eat it here," he says.

After much debate, I give up, pull out the food, and chomp away, while staring at the blue lines on the parking lot floor. That *bella* Italia certainly is devilish today.

We finish our "meal," scratch ourselves everywhere the mosquitoes have attacked, and go to Anna and Francesco's for dessert. They warmly greet us and recall my father's kindness in driving them around Toronto. They give us a full and conclusive tour of their apartment, and afterward we enjoy a typical dessert from Naples, a rum baba, a rich cake saturated in rum and filled with homemade pastry cream.

Arezzo—"just another old town"

Next, we take Tata to visit Robert, an American man who lives across our valley. He bought and completely renovated a house and its vast surrounding property. He has hundreds of olive trees on the hillsides around his home and has planted more than a thousand rosebushes. His water bill costs more than our rent each month. He has spent hundreds of thousands on the exterior stonework alone. Thus, the place is quite impressive.

Being extremely hospitable, he invites us to join him on one of his many stone patios for a beer. My dad, suddenly in no hurry, sits down on a teak chair. Dozens of large hand-made terra-cotta pots overflow with colorful flowers. An enchanting atmosphere prevails, as the candles flicker and the fire pit radiates a warm glow. The views are expansive, and we see lights across the valley, sparkling on the hillside.

"This is really good," my dad says.

"Yes, Robert has done an amazing job here," I say.

"I was talking about the beer," my dad says. "It's really nice and cold."

I smile, now recognizing that a "good atmosphere" for my dad depends on the quality and the price of beer. He should be quite content here for the next few hours, as Robert's hospitality is never ending.

We remain at Robert's for a long while, talking, laughing, and soaking up the "good atmosphere."

I hope that tomorrow will be a day of rest, because apparently, "If you've seen one old town, you've seen them all."

Chapter 5

Mischievous *Bella* Italia

Cortona sits majestically on top of a hillside. The colors of the ancient town contrast perfectly with the shimmering silver green of the olive groves and the dark green of the pines. A patch of sunlight shines on the scene like a large spotlight. I'm in the mood to go to Cortona tonight, and I tempt Tata with a cold beer. He is game, despite Cortona being "just another old town."

Some people maintain that Cortona is too touristy. I hate to say it, but there really are no undiscovered places in Italy. With the passing of a couple of thousand years, they have all been discovered, and some places don't warrant a return. Some travelers desire a vacation "off the beaten track," but I know from firsthand experience that one can then end up in an unsightly suburb. Tourists go where it is nice: towns filled with charming shops, quaint cafés, and good restaurants. Lovely forested areas with no tourists abound in Tuscany, but do Canadians want to fly all the way across the ocean to see trees?

Thus, off to Cortona we go. It's a beautiful town with medieval architecture and steep, narrow streets. At an elevation of two thousand feet, it embraces a view of the whole of Valdichiana.

After slaving all day, with my father astonished at how tired I get, I suggest we go out for dinner. I inform my father of our plans, and he agrees.

"We will go to a nice restaurant, so please put on some dressy clothes."

Thankfully, my sister Vesna had told me of my father's unwillingness to pack anything remotely formal. Forewarned, I am forearmed. I went to the market in Camucia prior to his arrival and purchased items my father would consider contraband, such as a crisp white shirt.

Shortly after seven, I knock on his door. "Are you ready?" I ask, opening the door slowly.

"Yes, I've been ready for a half hour," he states, in the tone of a man who lives by "time is money" and who has been kept waiting.

He exits, and I almost fall over, convulsed with laughter. He is wearing short shorts, of the Daisy Duke variety, with mid-ankle black socks and his cherished Chinese flip-flops. To his credit, his shorts do match the occasional splatter of gray paint on his flip-flops.

"I told you we're going out for a nice dinner and to dress up," I say.

He looks down. "That's why I put my black socks on."

He laughs hysterically and I join him, realizing he has single-handedly just redefined *la bella figura* ("making a good impression"). Giorgio Armani, move over!

After a bit of prodding, Tata dons the white shirt with a pair of long pants, though his beloved flip-flops stay put. We are about to leave when he says, "I forgot something." He goes back into his room and emerges with a white baseball cap and a broad smile. At least, the white cap matches the white shirt.

We head to Cortona, elegantly dressed, sort of. David drops us off and parks the car, while my dad and I watch the well-heeled in town. Undoubtedly, they're watching us as well.

The town is at its best. Terra-cotta vases overflowing with flowers line the main street, and candles shimmer in glass lanterns outside restaurants. We watch a pretty woman, who, despite all efforts to walk elegantly, trudges clumsily in four-inch heels across the ancient cobblestone. I fear she may stumble, though a streak of naughtiness thinks it would be amusing. She is dressed to the nines, in a black-sequined dress and delicate lace adorning her shoulders. She looks quite diva-like, in between steps. We catch a whiff of her strong, sweet perfume as she makes her way to the theater for the Tuscan Sun Festival. She is obviously on display, so we stare.

The air is abuzz with excitement, as men in smart dark suits and women in formal wear scurry to their events. Tourists who are not attending the festival stroll in the square. We guess people's nationalities before they speak:

Italians, by their tremendous sense of style. Germans, with their affinity for bright colors and comfortable sandals. American men, not even attempting to hide their desire to be comfortable all over, and the British are fair skinned, making them easy to pick out.

An Italian couple sits on the bench next to us with their screaming baby. Apologetic for interrupting our peace, they explain that she is hungry. The baby, suddenly distracted, looks at two older ladies passing by. They play with her, and she seems to have forgotten her hunger, her blue eyes shining, her dark black hair forming ringlets around her happy face. We smile at her, waving and cooing. I'm slightly jealous, looking at this sweet baby in a pretty summer dress, bringing so much pleasure to others.

Abruptly, as if remembering her hunger, she begins squirming and screaming at the top of her lungs, while her mother frantically gets the bottle of milk ready. My tinge of envy is gone.

David has found us, thanks to my dad's white baseball cap. The square is full of tourists, with more English and German being spoken than Italian. We walk past a couple, and with their thick American accents, they greet us, *buonasera*. We greet them with the same, in our own thick Canadian accents. An enterprising clothing shop has a sign declaring a one-euro entrance fee. A few doors down, a sign states that entrance is free to that shop.

We walk through the narrow cobblestone streets, admiring the ancient stone homes, the small gardens, and the pots of bright red geraniums on the doorsteps. My dad, meanwhile, examines menus.

We find a reasonable place to eat *and* drink and enjoy a pleasant evening out.

"This is also a good atmosphere," my dad says, cradling a large, cold beer in his hands.

I try to take a picture of my dad, but after several attempts I settle on one in which the expression on his face does not denote extreme torture but merely as if someone is pinching him hard. Perhaps the only way to have him smile in a photo is to turn it upside down.

We walk back to our car through the Parterre gardens, a beautiful park lined with lime trees. There is a public bathroom with a silver door leading to a chamber. A sign advises that for thirty cents, you can have up to fifteen minutes in there.

Happy and content, we are ready to go home and have a late-night grappa.

The smug look on our faces disappears when we discover our car battery is drained. We stand on the road, hoping to flag down someone. However, we are parked on a sharp curve and can only watch drivers speed past us in their fancy cars. As people approach the parking lot, David runs up to them, and they glare at him with suspicion.

Soon it becomes evident that no one carries jumper cables, including us. Several foreigners suggest we call a tow service and then, possibly judging by our car and/or my dad's flip-flops, add, "Of course, you will have to pay for this service."

We finally encounter an expert on jump-starting cars. This elegant Italian and his well-dressed, high-heeled girlfriend help us push the car while David is at the wheel, willing the engine to start. Despite our best efforts, there was not enough momentum.

Our Italian hero is undeterred. "In reverse," he commands.

We follow him, pushing the car the other way. Within seconds, we hear the Ferrari-like sound that I will no longer take for granted.

"*Grazie mille!* ['a thousand thanks']," we gratefully say.

"*Di niente!* ['It's nothing!'],*"* they insist.

David is thrilled and takes full advantage of the situation, maintaining that he needs to recharge the battery. I close my eyes and brace myself, not sure which is the lesser of two evils: the car having started or not. The anxious look on my father's face reveals that he feels the same way. We get home in record time, and I bid Mario Andretti a good night. The Slow Movement apparently exists here, but that impish *bella* Italia just won't let me in on it.

Chapter 6

Tata "Sees" Florence

Several days have passed since Tata's arrival, and soon it will be time for him to depart. David's chess game has improved. Tata now takes up to seven minutes before he says, "Check mate." Meanwhile, I have perfected how to make and serve oatmeal.

My mother had given my father a book describing the reign of the Medici family. Thus, a visit to Italy would not be complete without seeing Florence, once the throne of the Medici Empire.

I would like to do some shopping but fear (a) that I will have my dad with me and (b) that many of the stores will be closed at this time of year.

I love Florence, for it manages to be grand and yet quaint. I suppose this is the magic of Florence. I hope it will be equally as charming with David and my father, because I won't have free rein to spend outrageous sums on frivolous items, such as peach coats that do not keep one warm. I smile at my husband, squeeze his hand tightly, and, with only slight fondness, remember my good old single days.

Within minutes, I am reminded of why my sister's first Italian lesson after meeting David was *occhio alla strada* ("eyes on the road"). Not only does David have a need for continuous eye contact when speaking with someone, but he must also verify information in our guide book, examine the map, show my dad exactly where the free parking is, and plan our entire day, all while driving. Again, I fondly recall my single days and the train gently pulling into the station.

We enter Florence and soon notice we are the closest things to Italians here. Chinese, Moroccans, Africans, and Americans abound—everyone but Italians.

Africans are selling knockoff purses, sunglasses, and other wares. Suddenly, there is a domino effect, as each African gathers his sheet, warns the next guy, and scatters off, while two uniformed *carabinieri* with an aura of importance slowly stroll down the street. Minutes after they pass, the sheets are back on the ground, the knockoff bags placed on top, and everyone is back in business.

I look up at the grandeur of the Duomo. My father, meanwhile, is staring at his shoes. I tell him to look up at the Duomo. He reluctantly does, but I swear I hear him say, 'Just another church.'

As I contemplate the wonders of the Duomo and my father, the wonders of his shoes, I hear, "Hey, Ivanka!" Mary Angela, a young woman we had met in Florence years ago, recognizes me.

"Ciao! How are you?" I ask and greet her with a double kiss. "This is my father—" but he has vanished. Panicked, I look for him and find him a few feet away, hidden behind a group of tourists. I introduce him to Mary Angela, who warmly greets him.

My dad forces a smile, barely acknowledging her, then looks down at his shoes. I hope Mary Angela's eyes won't follow his.

We chat a bit, while my dad ducks out of the conversation.

He soon rejoins us and seems transformed; he is very charming, inquiring about her life in Florence. He poses for some pictures and even smiles.

We part ways, promising to be in touch soon.

"Is she gone?" my dad asks.

"Yes, why?" I say.

Relieved, he opens his mouth wide, takes out his teeth, puts them back in his pocket, and chuckles. Meanwhile, I can barely walk in my high heels and am sweltering, because I wore a pretty, fitted polyester dress, all to feel elegant while visiting chic Florence. The irony hits me, and so I laugh, too.

Despite being accompanied by two men, I still cling to the fantasy of doing some shopping. I desire another prized possession from Florence, albeit a much cheaper one. We will be visiting Canada in a few months, and I want to show up with something that screams, "Italy!" Because breast augmentation is out of the question, I hope to find something terribly fashionable.

My dream of purchasing a cherished item diminishes as we walk by shop after shop, with signs stating, *Chiuso per ferie* ("closed for holidays"). David and my father are overjoyed. As we approach the Duomo Tower, an Italian has left a note on the wall: "I drive across the country to get here and you're closed—thanks!"

Some people are still into making money, though, because two tour guides are in the square. Despite the heat, one is dressed in a heavy medieval outfit in red and gold, with pointy shoes and a hat to match. Sweltering, he attempts to explain the history of an ancient building to a group of hot, tortured-looking tourists. Another group of tourists a few feet away has gone high tech, and the leader drowns out the first guide with her microphone. They begin to compete, the guy in the red suit, with a face to match, speaking louder, and the woman with the microphone doing the same.

The Piazza della Signoria has been the center of political life in Florence since the fourteenth century. The prominent Palazzo Vecchio overlooking the square teems with tourists and the occasional well-dressed Italian.

A security guard is on a mission in the graceful Loggia dei Lanzi, an open-air sculpture gallery, designed in 1376. The statue of Perseus holding Medusa's head is a stark reminder of what happened to those who crossed the Medici, and it appears the same fate may await a German tourist. The guard takes his job of safeguarding the statues very seriously. He has a gun and pounces on unsuspecting tourist after tourist. His eyes rove about, eager to catch the next offender. A German is caught in the clandestine act of attempting to bring a bottle of Sprite into the area. The tourist insists it is filled with water, but the security man points to the bottle and accusingly says, "*Sprite, zucchero!*" ("Sprite, sugar!"). The tenaciousness of this German is as astonishing as his attachment to the bottle of Sprite. Refusing to leave it behind, he is denied entry. Satisfied, the guard moves on to his next victim. In all of our years here, we have yet to see anyone work with such fervor.

"If I ever open a security company, he will be the first guy I hire," David says.

Watching this energetic man has worn us out, and with the little strength we have left, we make one last stop at Piazzale Michelangelo. The square, dedicated to the great Renaissance sculptor Michelangelo, houses a replica of the *David*, set on a large pedestal, decorated with allegorical statues depicting day, night, dusk, and dawn. These copies are cast in bronze, while the originals are carved in white marble. The monument was carried to this location by nine pairs of oxen in 1873.

The views embrace the heart of Florence and the river Arno, with the Tuscan hills providing a scenic backdrop. With the sun setting in the distance, an American couple enjoys a romantic picnic amid a flood of tourists. They have arranged some appetizers on a pretty tablecloth and are toasting each other with champagne, as if they're only ones here.

Exhausted, we head home. Tata will be leaving tomorrow and will be able to say that he "'saw" a lot on his trip to Italy. Despite its grandeur and majestic views, however, Florence did not prove to be one of his favorite places; the beer was simply too expensive.

The next day we drop him off at the train station, and with regret I say goodbye. We wave, while my father yells out the window, "See you next year!"

I smile, thinking, *Maybe the flip-flops will wear out by then.* Or maybe not, if rascally *bella* Italia gets her way.

Chapter 7

Back to School

I automatically wake up at seven and feel a deep sadness that my father is not here to offer suggestions on how to prepare oatmeal. I miss him and hope he comes back soon. Perhaps Italian family values are rubbing off on me. If so, that's a good thing.

The long, hot, lazy days of summer have given way to a flourish of fall activities. Farmers gather their crops, while their wives get their households ready for winter. Tourists leave, and children return to school. I'm reminded of this as I receive a text: "Hello, one of our teachers is sick. Would you be able to help us out with tomorrow evening's lessons? A kiss."

David looks at the text, grimaces, and says, "No."

He has been permanently scarred. He refers to his brief teaching stint at Kids' Summer Camp as "the hardest job I have ever had." By comparison, he fondly recalls re-shingling his roof beneath the scorching sun, doing heavy construction, hustling as a bus boy under the watchful eye of a demanding boss, apprenticing for a crazed cabinetmaker, wrestling crocodiles, fighting gladiators, and so on.

Thus, as a loving husband, he tries to shield me from what will likely prove hazardous to my health. Everyone knows that when a wife is happy, so is her husband. More than a decade of marriage has taught him a thing or two.

I feel sorry for the director of the school and recall her willingness to verify that I have no business teaching English. And so I repress my memories of being bullied by eight-year-olds at Kids' Summer Camp. David, wiser, or perhaps blessed with a better memory, suggests I do it this time but say that I cannot do it on a regular basis, thereby limiting my exposure to the little terrorists and delaying my ultimate demise.

I survive, if only barely, the one night.

Weeks pass, with all of the teachers the epitome of good health. I relax and spend my days as I imagined them: I sleep in, take glorious walks through our valley, write stories, and cook fabulous meals. I take a *pausa* each afternoon and revel in *la dolce vita*. I learn it is possible for me to unwind.

Then the call comes. "We are desperate! All of the teachers are sick, so I would need you to teach for three hours." A pause and in a lower tone she adds, "Children's classes."

Having lived the sweet life for a time, I've let my memories of the "little darlings" fade sufficiently to reply, "Sure, I'll be there tomorrow afternoon."

David overhears my conversation and stares at me in shock.

"It's only three hours. I will live to tell the tale," I say, convincing neither myself nor David.

I wake early the next morning to prepare the evening's lessons. The three groups are at different levels, so, before I know it, I've spent most of the day and my Internet plan preparing the classes. I refrain from figuring out what I'm earning per hour. Worse still, because I'll be teaching in a couple of hours, I forfeit my glass of wine with lunch—though for one fleeting moment I contemplate bringing the bottle with me.

I arrive early, and so do my first two students. One is the hyperactive only child from last year. I shudder. The other student, a ten-year-old girl, with siblings, is well behaved and polite.

I begin with a clothesline project. They draw, then color and cut out various articles of clothing to hang on a string and label in English. After a few meager articles of clothing they lose interest, letting me know, in no uncertain terms, "*Che noioso!*" ("How boring!")

I don't give up but urge them on, calling them names of famous designers, hoping they will suddenly get inspired. Because even little Italians are preoccupied with *la bella figura,* this works like a charm. In no time, the dresses have polka dots, and even socks are no longer monochromatic but have curious designs on them.

"Giorgio Armani!" I chant, hoping these ten-year-olds have heard of him.

Miraculously, they have, thanks to parenting skills that stress the importance of designer goods. The skirts sport jagged hems, and stitching adorns the sides and the bottom. The creative Italian blood is flowing. The clothesline project is a success, though they probably won't remember the English word for a single article of clothing minutes after they leave. I have filled the allotted hour by going down memory lane with the names of elderly and possibly long dead Italian designers. They pick up their clotheslines and run off to their doting parents.

The next group of boys is a harder sell, because they balk at the mere suggestion of the clothesline project. Thankfully, I have a back-up plan involving flashcards. They start to have fun—a bit too much—and are soon without constraint. I watch the clock.

My final group consists of the live wires from last year. This hour will be the most daunting one. As they walk into the classroom and spot me, instead of their regular teacher, their eyes grow wide. Eight-year-old Francesco exclaims, "You grew your hair! I like it better."

I reply in English, and they both sigh and in unison moan, "*Oh, Dio!*"

As I speak English, they stare at me as if they have sighted a UFO, asking each other, "What is she saying?"

"If you'd pay more attention in English class, you would know," I say.

Despite not understanding a word, they howl in a fit of laughter. I explain that their regular teacher is absent because she has a cold.

Francesco rolls his large eyes and, lacking compassion, says, "Give me a break. I have a cold, too, and I am still here."

Alessandro explains, "He loves her!"—which is the point where Francesco jumps on him, and they start fighting.

I sigh loudly. Alarmed, as if only now noticing my presence, Francesco calms down and nonchalantly asks, "How old are you, and are you married?"

Alessandro remembers my husband from Kids' summer camp and says, "She is married to the *signore* from camp."

"Yes, I am. Is he handsome?" I ask, not expecting a response.

"Yes," answers Francesco, seriously.

Alessandro, meanwhile, smiles weirdly and says, "I would like to show you something." His shoves his finger, with a nail barely attached, in my face.

I let out a shriek, encouraging him to gross me out, on and off, for the rest of the lesson. I try to control them, but each time I turn my back to write on the blackboard, they disappear. One hides under the desk, the other makes a break for the supply room. Fifteen minutes with these two already seems like an eternity.

I remember David's trick from summer camp—not the one where he threatened to call the police, but his other plan for controlling the children: bribing them. This should be beneath me, but desperate times call for desperate measures. "If you finish this project, you can play your favorite game."

"Okay, but any game we want," barters Francesco.

Though fearing what this game could entail, I nonetheless concede. Designer names do nothing for them; their parents have not taken Italian parenting seriously. Their clotheslines are finished, both equally worthy of the worst taste in design award.

"*Oh, Dio,*" they moan, when I give them a worksheet as review. They refuse to complete it until I choose "whose clothes are better."

After I make a sizable contribution in helping them with the worksheet, they argue over who is the winner.

"You had more help than me!"

"No, she helped you more!"

Another round of fighting breaks out.

"I am the winner. I am the only one who knows any English around here!" I say. This outburst quiets them in the nick of time. I pull out their favorite game, and moments after they start playing, their parents arrive. They urge the boys to get ready, but the boys refuse to leave. To their parents' delight, it appears there is nowhere else their "little darlings" would rather be than at their English lesson. Although there is somewhere else *I'd* rather be.

Certain I won't be returning, with relief I enjoy the drive home through the beautiful Tuscan countryside, singing along to passionate arias playing on the radio.

A roaring fire greets me, and I hurry to get dinner ready. An Italian prince's empathy only goes so far. He redeems himself, as he pours me a large glass of red wine and awaits my war stories.

Chapter 8

Italian History—Like It or Not

Martha Stewart must be a fraud. I'm not referring to the issue with the securities exchange—no, that provided countless hours of entertainment, as talk show hosts posted photos of how she would redecorate her cell. That little indiscretion proved far too amusing. I'm referring to her smug smile as she welcomed twenty guests who have all arrived simultaneously—and early. The same smile that inspires the rest of us mere mortals to foolishly think we can do it, too. Her table is set with fresh flowers, the candles are lit, and her hair is freshly washed and styled, while fragrant aromas waft from the oven.

Decades older than me, Martha Stewart bursts with positive energy. And while elderly Italian women possess the same vigor, at least their tables aren't decorated with flowers or candles. Such items are reserved only for the cemetery.

It's October, but we are blessed with a warm, sunny day. Therefore, David is outside setting up our "terrace" area. He randomly places several tables outside and covers them in long white tablecloths, as in a small restaurant. Wild flowers from around the property and olive branches complete the table arrangements. With views of the hilltop town of Castiglion Fiorentino and the vast fields surrounding the "terrace," it's an enchanting setting. David is carrying chairs from the cantina when the first cars pull into our driveway.

I look at the clock, panicked, and down at myself. They are a half hour early! I sigh, because this isn't the type of crowd that will sit in the living room with an appetizer and a cocktail, while I finish up in the kitchen. As they enter, I smile graciously at the half-dozen Italian women and men who will soon be hovering over me. I excuse myself and steal away to the bathroom, where I give my dry shampoo one chance to miraculously transform the state of my hair. I return, vowing never to buy the product again, and endeavor to finish the meal with the "help" of several women closely supervising.

Despite living in Italy for years, I'm still not prepared for the *più o meno* ("more or less") formula, with guests staggering their arrival, either too early or too late. I always resemble the Bride of Frankenstein with pink lipstick when company arrives. More maniacal beeping is heard, as guests announce their arrival to us and the entire village. Large quantities of dessert and *spumante* are handed to me. Italians are truly generous.

One by one, they enter the house and are duly impressed. They love the exterior stonework and the extensive private grounds. The house also boasts three sizable bedrooms, two bathrooms, a large eat-in kitchen, and a living room.

"How much do you pay for rent?" asks Elisa.

"Five hundred and fifty euros a month," I say, expecting accolades.

"What?" she says. "That is way too much!"

Italians have one of the highest home ownership rates in all of Europe. This could be in large part due to parents building enough additions to their own homes to house a small community, but regardless.

"Why don't you buy this house and stop paying rent?" Elisa asks, and everyone awaits my reply.

"It would cost a fortune. A mortgage would be two and half thousand euros a month."

They reflect for a moment, then add, "But at least you would own this home!"

"Where do I come up with the extra two thousand euros a month?" I ask.

They ponder the gravity of our situation and arrive at a solution: we can pack our bags and move out of this overpriced house, with its beautiful grounds and privacy, into a teeny apartment in a nearby town. It makes perfect sense, in the enigmatic Italian mind.

"But we don't want to live there," I say.

That is beside the point. The fact that we don't have the desire to amass real estate on our demise is of little consequence.

Everyone joins the debate—except me, knowing better.

More beeping. Our previous landlord, Rocco, has arrived.

"Permesso?" ("Permission?"), he asks. Without waiting for a reply, he enters and gives his nod of approval.

"Looking at this place from the outside, I didn't think it was much, but from the inside it is incredible!" he says.

David and I are perplexed, because the home's beauty lies in its exterior stonework, which our landlords had paid a fortune to redo. There are more than twenty acres with forty pine trees adorning the grounds. Rose bushes and oleanders abound. If fully restored, the house would be more than five thousand square feet.

Rocco joins the heated debate on our home ownership and, when he finds out how much we pay in rent, shakes his head in disbelief. "You are paying way too much."

David rolls his eyes at me, as the same thought occurs to both of us. Ironically, Rocco charged us the same amount for a small one-bedroom, one-bathroom house, complete with his mother-in-law sleeping in the room next door, snoring so loudly we thought she had joined us in our bed.

Rocco continues giving free advice in the form of a sermon, in a thick Neapolitan dialect that triggers his daughters to yell, "Speak Italian." He obediently does, making a concentrated effort for a few sentences. He lectures us on "the futility of throwing money away on rent," and I preferred it when I didn't understand what he was saying.

I suggest they go relax on the terrace, but everyone, except David and me, is too embroiled in the debate. Finally, the state of our finances is postponed, as most of the invited and uninvited guests turn up. Simona brought her parents, because she was sure we must be dying to meet them. Rosanna thought we would find her cousin charming. Elisa brought a friend for her son to play with.

I nudge David, and he gets the hint: *Get everyone out of my kitchen before I have a nervous breakdown!* He escorts the majority of the guests out, but some stay behind to "help me." I answer simultaneous questions, while dodging several people who hinder my path to the fridge, the stove, and the sink.

In an attempt to remove them from my work area, I show them David's work portfolio. "This is what David made when we lived in Canada."

The portfolio displays photos of high-end furniture with inlay, carving, and so on. David had worked for a renowned cabinetmaker, Michael Fortune, and several of his exclusive designs are featured. They hastily flip through the pages and, minutes later, come back to the kitchen.

However, the simple shelves installed on our wall that required virtually no skill and only basic tools intrigue them. "Did David make these?"

"Yes, he did," I say.

Now they are impressed. "This is great work!" They value the *Arte Povere* style. We will have to keep this secret from Michael Fortune.

I am saved by the bell, as the phone rings. Some guests are lost. "Can you drive out to meet us?" asks Paolo.

"Where are you? Did David send you the directions?"

"Yes, he did, but we are not using them. We don't need them."

Evidently, you do! is what I want to reply, but instead I yell outside to David to take the call.

The car starts, and David peels out.

I think of Martha Stewart, chatting with guests while cooking complicated menus at her kitchen island, whereas I cannot keep track of how many tomatoes I sliced, with Rocco still on a rampage because we pay too much rent.

I want to throw everyone out, double-bolt the entrance, and install a cat door to slip the food out, plate by plate. Then, while the guests eat, I will take a shower, blow-dry my hair until it is completely dry, apply lots of dark eye makeup, and emerge, with a martini glass in hand and a welcoming, if not crazed, smile. To complete the look, I will make my entrance wearing a tiara.

Back to reality, I shuffle through the throngs of unfamiliar people in the kitchen. No one ever gets out of my way but only allows me to circumvent him or her momentarily. I continue cooking and arranging dishes, now with a somewhat demented smile.

Finally, and miraculously, everything is ready, and it is time to move the party outside. David is just returning with the guests in tow.

Simona sees the "patio" with direct views of the hilltop town and says, "How incredible that so many years ago someone had the foresight to put it right here, with this gorgeous view."

Laughing to myself, I refrain from letting her know that it is actually a *concimaia*, where the pig manure was stored to season before use in the fields. Thus, the dinner table is sitting on an ex–manure heap.

Our "terrace trattoria"

Everyone hovers over the food table, loudly conversing. Enrico is also there to provide scintillating conversation for himself.

Greta, an adorable two-and-half-year-old, announces, *"Qui e bellisimo!"* ("It's beautiful here!")

I taste the potato salad and realize the "chives" I had freshly gathered from our field and sprinkled on top for that "Martha Stewart" touch are, in fact, grass. My Martha Stewart herb-picking lessons will need refining. No one else seems to notice. Perhaps they mistake it for an American specialty food item.

They sample my broccoli salad and are amazed. When they first noticed the broccoli was not cooked, they all protested that "broccoli is not to be eaten raw." But now they are giving me the "highest compliment" by saying, "This is *actually* very good."

Enrico, meanwhile, has cornered his latest unsuspecting victim and is pontificating, beginning with the year 1200. Enrico is an elderly man, about eighty, who lives down the road. His family owned most of the area, and it's rumored that he is filthy rich. Judging by the cheap, almost undrinkable wine he has brought, he plans to keep the wealth in the family.

His first prey manages to break free, and now David is trapped. He looks at me with a silent plea for help. I smile innocently and feign urgent work in the kitchen, unable to endure the next eight hundred years of history.

After three hundred years, David joins me in the kitchen. He has brought in a stack of platters and washes them by hand, something *I* usually do *after* the guests leave. Hence, this is his devious escape plan. Meanwhile, Enrico, not wanting to deprive David of five hundred precious years of Italian history, hobbles in and attaches himself to David by the sink. David is held captive, as Enrico persists with his spirited ramblings.

Enrico, on occasion, asks a question, albeit a rhetorical one that he immediately answers in elaborate detail, but for that fleeting millisecond there is a glimmer of hope in David's eyes that Enrico will stop and let him speak.

To ensure that the person Enrico is lecturing still has a pulse, every so often Enrico asks, "So, you understand what I am saying, right?"

David responds with frightened eyes, having been caught. He clears his throat several times, hoping Enrico will take the indiscernible sound to mean: "Yes, of course, how fascinating, the Medicis, 1531."

Enrico, though no fool, is forgiving and will give David several chances to redeem himself. To ensure that David has not missed out on a pertinent part of Florentine history, Enrico backs up to the start of the Medici rule in 1434.

Meanwhile, in a lively voice Marina describes her recent encounter with the police. "They almost gave me a ticket. I begged them not to!" Her crime? *Not* passing on a blind curve and thus causing a long traffic jam. "I told them

I could not see ahead to safely pass the *ape* [a mini-truck on three wheels]. Their harsh reply: 'We are sure there was some point at which you could have passed, had you wanted to.' Seeing I was on the verge of tears, they let me off with a warning. Only in Italy!" she says and looks at me for sympathy.

She certainly has mine, but most of the men in the room are siding with the police.

As everyone finishes eating lunch and the afternoon turns to evening, I realize that neither Martha Stewart nor any of her contemporaries have written a book on how to get rid of guests. Volumes exist on how to impress them, how to keep them entertained, but as dinnertime approaches and no one goes home, a manual on how to encourage guests to leave might be in order.

Roberta and Barbara, our hens, have been very productive, thus I whip up some devilled eggs and pasta with tomato sauce. David, almost back in our century now, takes this opportunity to run to the *cantina* and cut prosciutto. No doubt, Enrico will offer to "help," but maybe David can outrun him.

We carry out all of the improvised food, and this time I refrain from any decorative garnishes that involve grass.

I take Greta to see the hens, sleeping on their stoop. She runs to them and hugs Barbara hard, refusing to let go. The stunned hens look up, then close their eyes and go back to sleep. Greta, fearless, wants to stay with the hens. I pry her away, with the promise that she can come back to play with them during the day.

Midnight approaches, and finally our guests, and their guests, begin to depart. We say goodnight, and they thank us profusely, stopping at regular intervals. Rosanna gives me two kisses, thanks me, and says, "I love you!"

The Canadian me wants to say, "That's nice," but I do manage an enthusiastic *Grazie!*

We wave as they drive away, and, despite the late hour, they joyfully honk goodbye several times, with more frantic waving and blowing of kisses. The Italians really do excel at living and enjoying the small pleasures of the present: family, friends, food, and even, on this occasion, bad wine.

Meanwhile, I am completely worn out, and, although it was fun, I swear to David that I cannot do this again. I simply do not have the stamina of an Italian *signora* in her eighties or of Martha Stewart.

Chapter 9

Roundabout Ruckus

Another day begins under the glorious Tuscan sun. I lazily awaken to a multitude of birds chirping and the occasional squawk of a pheasant at home in our fields. The day is warm, and the atmosphere, relaxed. I abandon my *casalinga* look and dress in chic Italian clothes, complete with ridiculously high heels. I am ready for a day of shopping and visiting friends in Arezzo. David also sheds his farm clothes and dons slim-fit pants, paired with a crisp white shirt and a pair of Prada shoes an Italian friend had given him. Those who like to envision us happily sipping Chianti under the Tuscan sun would be satisfied. Today, our life looks like an Italian commercial.

We drive through our valley, with its hillsides turning golden yellow and vineyards with autumn-orange leaves adorning the landscape. The day is seemingly perfect.

We take the main road that leads from Cortona to Arezzo, and, within minutes, the integrity of our brakes and seatbelts is tested. An ancient Fiat Panda, complete with elderly couple, the driver only slightly taller than the dashboard, has pulled out onto the road, as if our car speeding toward them were invisible. Naturally, within seconds, David passes, slowing down to get a look at the culprit. The old man stares ahead, oblivious, while I worry about oncoming traffic.

We enter the suburban outskirts of Arezzo and approach my nemesis: the roundabout. The posted speed is 30 kilometers (18 miles), but everyone enters as if a Formula One racer. I brace myself, for our turn is next.

My body hurls forward from the blow. With a lifetime of driving in

Canada, I have not experienced so much as a tap, but this is already our second accident here. We exit the car, and the *signora* apologizes. We survey our sturdy twenty-two-year-old car and see no damage. Her plastic bumper, however, is completely smashed. Because there is no damage to us or our car, the *signora* is anxious to part ways.

Prior to letting the offender sneak away, David fortuitously inspects our car to ensure that all is in order. It won't start.

"That has nothing to do with the accident. You are having engine trouble, and that is *not* my fault!" protests the previously sweet, concerned *signora*.

We are blocking rush-hour traffic in one of Arezzo's main roundabouts. The *signora* refuses to accept this accident as her responsibility. We risk our lives, as we stand in the middle of the roundabout with cars racing around us.

"We drove here from Castiglion Fiorentino and have not had any trouble with the engine prior to this," David says. "Something must have been knocked out of place. It was a rather hard blow."

Discovering we are from the same town, she softens and tells me about her shop in town. She stops mid sentence, as she catches herself, and returns to business. "It is absolutely not my fault," she says, convinced.

We are reluctant to call the police, for after our last accident they were obliged to call the closest tow truck company, which came complete with a crazed mechanic. The incident took years off our lives.

We have no choice but to call the *carabinieri*, for we don't want to be stuck with a one hundred euro tow-truck bill, plus the cost of fixing the engine. The *signora* offers to phone them and, with a warning smile, adds, "My husband is a *carabiniere*."

Knowing this, we fear we may end up accused of being at fault, even though we were rear-ended.

The local police spot us and drive over. The *signora* ushers them away, saying, "No need for you, the *carabinieri* will be here any moment."

The local police, glad not to have been inconvenienced, wave goodbye and drive off, leaving us to wait for one of her husband's best friends to arrive.

Morning rush-hour traffic crawls past us. I call Rosanna, the friend we were meeting, and she drives over. She parks her car illegally within the roundabout, further blocking traffic. She is aware of my anxiety on the roads here, hence comforts me: "I've personally been in so many accidents; it's a normal part of life. The important thing is that no one was hurt."

We've already had two accidents here, several near misses, and apparently many more are to come! My paranoia is becoming justified.

Two other friends from Arezzo spot us. They, too, park their car illegally and run to our aid. Our posse surrounds us, while the *signora* mutters, "It really is not my fault."

The *carabinieri* arrive and, after surveying the scene, seem rather bored by this mere fender bender.

The *signora* quickly says, "I slowly entered the circle."

"No one in Italy ever drives slowly," I say.

"He braked suddenly, and that is why I hit them," she says, shifting the blame.

"There was an ambulance coming through, so I didn't enter the circle, but I did *not* slam on my brakes," David explains.

From the position of the cars, it's clear that he's telling the truth. The traffic moves at a snail's pace, while the policeman helps us fill out the paperwork. David intermittently keeps trying to get the car to start; it refuses to.

The other policeman lets me in on how bad the drivers are here. "You would not believe how many accidents take place each day. The minute it rains, forget it. No one knows how to drive any longer."

My friends wish they could shush him, though he does have words of consolation for me: "There are many bad drivers here, but nothing compared to those in Naples."

My suspicions are confirmed: every Italian driver *is* out to get me!

Rosanna's husband, Andrea, parks his car illegally in the circle and joins our posse. The *carabiniere* notices and jovially says, "All these illegally parked cars better not cause any more accidents in the roundabout!" Then he laughs.

Only in Italy!

Andrea has a small green bag in his hand. "I brought tools. I'll see if I can fix your car."

Andrea is not a mechanic and possesses the finesse of a bull in a china shop. I fear for our car, and so does David, but Andrea insists and starts work on the car, while the *carabiniere* chats with us. We discuss life in Canada versus Italy, and we discover he has relatives in New York.

"I think I have solved the problem," Andrea says. "The air supply was knocked out of place, so I reattached it."

The *carabiniere*, who has been amicably chatting with us as if he has all the time in the world, becomes serious and decides to help. He gets in the car and revs the engine like a maniac, up to 7000 RPMs. The car roars. David's face shows obvious signs of distress. The *carabiniere* revs the engine hard several more times, almost inducing a heart attack in David.

The *signora* says that if all is in order, "There really is no need to send any of these documents," suggestive of guilt on her part, to the insurance agency. The *carabinieri* agree.

"Please visit my shop next time you are in town," she says and speeds off.

The *carabinieri* shake our hands, saying, "What a pleasure to meet you!" as if having been introduced to us at a cocktail party. Our friends return to their illegally parked cars, freeing the morning rush-hour traffic as they drive off.

Not a ticket was issued, no fines to be paid, no demerit points deducted, and no claim filed with any pesky insurance agency. All of this with the police present!

I get into our seemingly invisible car and buckle up.

Chapter 10

Home Invasion

David answers the phone. The conversation revolves around how many eggs Roberta and Barbara have been laying and their overall well-being, thus I know it is my mother-in-law, Maria, calling. Usually, after all of the animal anecdotes have been exhausted, just before hanging up, David says, "Yes, Ivanka is also fine." Ever since they gave us their two prized hens, I have learned to develop a thick skin. Admittedly, the hens are adorable.

Though our hens are still her number-one priority, the next matter of consequence is our garden and whether David will be planting any winter items. At this point, I can tell that my father-in-law, Giorgio, has taken over the phone, as David nods, with long interludes of silence as he listens to Giorgio lecture on planting a winter garden. Prior to saying goodbye, Giorgio makes his own inquiries as to the health and egg-production patterns of Roberta and Barbara. He does not ask about me.

Maria comes back to the phone, and the weather is discussed. This is an inexhaustible topic, for they not only analyze the temperature in our two parts of Italy—theirs in the beautiful mountainous area of Abruzzo and ours in Tuscany—but also deliberate on the weather patterns back in Toronto.

Finally, all urgent matters out of the way, Maria tells David, almost as if an afterthought, "Oh, by the way, we were robbed last night."

David, in shock, listens as his mother launches into a tirade about these "home invaders."

"So they came this morning to see if we are okay. Then they expect me to make coffee for them and offer them something to eat. I was in the middle of breakfast myself and never got to finish." Maria's rant continues for some time.

David is confused and interrupts, asking, "Who are you talking about?"

"Your *zia* and cousins!" she emphatically says.

It takes a moment to register, but it's apparent that Maria is far less bothered by the intruder who wandered through her bedroom in the middle of the night than with *Zia* in her kitchen first thing this morning.

Maria continues, "*Zia* naturally came to give us advice on alarms and on all the other things we should have done. She offers plenty of advice, though she knows nothing about it. And they came so early—"

David interrupts, "Are you okay? What did they take?"

Maria, slightly irritated by David's silly questions, says, "They took your father's two thousand euro watch, my gold watch and other jewelry, his wallet with about five hundred euros in cash, and, oh, yeah, a special EEE phone that belonged to your cousin, who happened to be helping us yesterday and slept over." She hopes David is satisfied with this report, because she is eager to return to the details of what she considers the real "home invasion."

"The important thing is that you didn't get hurt," David says.

"The important thing," she corrects David, "is that the burglar just took what he wanted and let us sleep in peace." It is obvious that the equally uninvited *Zia* and her sons, in contrast, interrupted Maria's breakfast and wouldn't leave her in peace.

The intruder was also considerate, in that he made no noise at all in the kitchen while feasting, as he helped himself to a glass of red wine, accompanied by a 36-month aged Parmigiano Reggiano from Parma.

David lets her rant for a while, then gets the rest of the details. The thief seemed to make himself right at home, strolling from one room to another and taking whatever he considered valuable. Something was pilfered from almost every room. Not satisfied with everything he took, the burglar then left Giorgio's pants, along with the cousin's briefcase, strewn across the lawn.

Incidentally, their dog, which never misses an opportunity to bark at a housefly and keeps David and me up for all hours during the night, did not peep as the home invader made his rounds. Perhaps the dog is not nearly as stupid as I had given him credit for. My in-laws maintain the dog was drugged.

The conversation concludes with David consoling Maria, telling her not to be too upset by the "home invasion," for he's certain that *Zia* and her sons had only the best of intentions.

"Yeah, whatever. Tell your wife we say hello," are Maria's final words.

Chapter 11

Rustic Times Call for Rustic Measures

I decide to go for my walk, while David awaits the plumber. The assumption is made that you are always at home, thus scheduling an actual day and time for his visit is unnecessary. This has gotten David out of a walk for three days now. Perhaps David is thankful for this assumption.

Despite running into the occasional wild boar, which quickly scurries away, I believe it's safe for me to go up the forested hill alone. Luciano assured me of this when we first arrived several years ago. In my heavily accented and broken Italian, I had asked whether it was safe to walk alone.

He replied, "You are safe. There are no foreigners here."

"We are foreigners," I replied.

"Yes, but you are the right type of foreigners," he assured me.

My walks keep me feeling young. It's not that I feel the physical benefits, but when you walk through a village where the inhabitants' average age is eighty, you are bound to feel young. Being called little *tesoro* ("treasure") by elderly Dario also helps. Norma, eighty-seven, has made homemade pasta and is drying it in her window. She, too, warmly greets me, referring to me as *cara,* "dear."

On my way home, I see a cat in the vineyard outside our front gate. He lies in the dirt without motivation, and each day thereafter, he looks at me with great disinterest, almost boredom. He never seems to move.

I check on him at various intervals during the day, but no matter what time it is, this cat never leaves his chosen spot under the vines. This is the place he has picked to die—albeit one of the most beautiful places on earth.

Moved with pity, I cannot let this happen outside our paradisiacal gates. He will have to try to get well. I am willing to help, and so is David. Though we love pets, due to our travel to Canada, we'd decided it was best not to have one. Yet this one chose us—well, sort of.

We name him Rusty, because his coat is reddish brown.

Each day we place bowls of warm milk and portions of our dinner at the end of our driveway, to try to nurse him back to health. He doesn't approach us and eats his meals only when left alone, after we are a considerable distance away.

Several days pass, and Rusty gets over his initial shyness and fear and cautiously comes to his bowl, with us still nearby. On closer inspection, we realize that a more appropriate name for Rusty would be *Rustico* or "Rustic." He can optimistically be described as half alive. In cat years, he must be at least one hundred. A more unattractive animal could never be found; his fur is matted, his claws are long and never retract, his ear is mangled and bleeding. He eats and drinks noisily, and he has a permanent surly gaze and a runny nose and occasionally goes into frightful sneezing fits. Notwithstanding, I am determined to try to love my new "pet."

It isn't long before I realize I've taken on more than I anticipated. Wishing he would leave, I recognize that I'm not as good a person as I'd previously thought. None of this matters to Rustico. He is determined to stay. He is going to become our "pet." Day by day, Rustico gets braver and moves closer and closer to us and to our front door.

Ironically, Giovanna, our neighbor, recently offered to give us their gorgeous cat, Matta, a real princess who gets away with plenty, due to her beauty. She would arrive each morning, have breakfast, and allow herself to be petted, then hop into her basket near the fireplace. If David happened to be in a chair next to her, she would extend her paw and place it on his arm. Then, when it suited her, she let us know that she wanted to leave. Noticing our deep affection for Matta, Giovanna offered to let us adopt her. However, we felt that we couldn't take on the responsibility.

Matta (meaning "crazy" in Italian)

Matta must have taken offense, because she hasn't been around for a few weeks. Instead, Rustico now sits outside, coughing and sneezing, like someone with a bad cold who has smoked a lifetime.

This poor creature is far sicker than we thought, and although we wish he would leave, we discover some goodness deep within us. We enlist the help of Giovanna, who often takes in stray cats and nurses them back to health.

Giovanna, who has seen plenty of rough-looking cats in her lifetime, winces as she gets a look at our "new cat." Getting over her initial shock, she politely says, "*Rustico* is a very fitting name. You need to take him to a vet. I know a good one who is not too expensive."

We wonder what "not too expensive" means to a cat lover. We had contemplated taking him to the vet but feared being responsible for what we were certain would be his inevitable fate.

"I can come with you. I need to bring two of my cats as well."

Motivated by recognition that it would be inhumane not to take this cat to the vet and not wishing to appear ruthless and coldhearted, we arrange to go to the vet together.

The next day we drive through the lovely Tuscan countryside with

Giovanna in the backseat, along with Rustico and her two cats. Rustico is the hero of the group, as he remains quiet in his cage, while the other two cats loudly meow in protest. The vet is only a half-hour away, but with the commotion from the cats, it seems like an eternity.

Soon there is an unbearable odor in the car. We open all of the windows and drive through the glorious Tuscan countryside, with noisy meowing and ghastly smells emanating from our car.

We arrive and fearfully open each cage, only to discover that Rustico is the culprit. David is less than amused, as he cleans up and vows never to have children.

We leave our name with the receptionist, and soon Rustico is called into the examination room. The vet thoroughly checks him, while we prepare for what we assume will be the tragic diagnosis.

Instead, the vet hooks him up to an I.V. drip and returns with a pile of papers and instructions and various boxes in her hand.

"You will have to get all of these prescriptions filled and carefully adhere to the directions. This cat has many illnesses and will need constant care," the vet says.

I now feel faint.

I look at the long list of medications and imagine just what "constant care" means. Hence, I ask, "Do you think the cat is suffering and if so . . ."

The vet flashes me a reproachful look. "This cat may have a few years left in him, *if* you will give him his medicine properly."

I look at the dozen or so prescriptions in her hand and envision my life revolving around caring for this poor sick cat.

Feebly, we begin to explain that while we feel badly for Rustico, he is not our cat. We just found him, and we travel often. The vet will hear no more. She hands us the pile of prescriptions and a bill and walks away, scowling.

We have no choice, so we take Rustico home, get the prescriptions filled, stock up on several more bottles of wine, and begin our days as caregivers.

We keep his basket at a distance in the garden, but each morning he chooses to sleep one step closer to our front door, aspiring to make his way in, eventually.

We invite our friend Laura, a cat lover, over for lunch, and instead of the customary bottle of wine or dessert one brings for the hostess, Laura brings goodies for Rustico: gourmet cat food and other treats. She has indeed spent a small fortune on him.

Rustico is enjoying all of this attention and puts on an even sadder, more forlorn look, as Laura dotes on him. Because Laura usually brings dessert, I haven't made any, so I whip up some crepes, while Laura stays with Rustico and talks to him soothingly. To get extra sympathy, Rustico launches into a sneezing fit. I just about gag.

Laura leaves us with a host of instructions about which gourmet tin he is to receive at what time and directives on how to get his fur shiny. Next thing we know, we are serving Rustico, hand and foot, feeding him the gourmet cat food intermittently with all of his medications, along with warm milk and a beaten egg yolk that will supposedly unmat his fur and make it shine.

In no time, Rustico will eat *only* the gourmet cat food, and the average-priced stuff we purchased will no longer do. Leftovers, good enough for me and David, are snubbed in favor of gourmet treats. Pasta is also out of the question, with or without meat sauce on it. We rename him Prince Rustico, as we wonder how on earth we got ourselves into this situation.

When the gourmet cat food runs out, I overhear David having a little chat with Rustico.

"Listen, pal, these are your choices; take it or leave it," David says, as he puts down the bowl of budget cat food. Prince Rustico sniffs it and decides to leave it. Laura would be appalled at us!

Despite Prince Rustico's lack of appreciation, each day David lovingly cares for the cat's wounded ear and gives him his long list of medicines. Giovanna has brought over a contraption that we put over Rustico's head, so he will not scratch his ear. With this on, he is more unsightly than ever.

After several weeks, Rustico appears only marginally better, despite the long list of medications and extreme care. We have been duped into buying the gourmet cat food for him that he devours like a wild hungry beast. The egg yolk whisked into warm milk daily that Laura swore would leave Rustico's fur shiny is not having the desired results. He still snarls at David and me, despite everything we do for him, and he recently bit David. We don't know how much more we can take. Our lives in Tuscany are not as charmed as most people imagine.

At last, we get our ticket out: we will be leaving for Canada soon, and we cannot ask anyone to take care of him. We look for an animal shelter we can take him to.

After much searching, we discover a group of animal lovers that will take in pets deemed healthy enough. First, you must take the animal to a vet, who determines whether Rustico will go to a cat lover, where he will live the remainder of his earthly days, or go to "cat heaven."

I call the organization and explain how we happened to acquire Rustico.

"Are you sure you want to give him up?" the voice asks soothingly, as if I am faced with a very difficult decision.

Because Rustico has swatted David for a second time and snarls at me every time I approach, I want to answer, "Yes, the sooner the better." Instead, I keep my wits about me and calmly answer, "Yes, we travel often, and, regretfully, we don't have *any* pets, due to this."

"Where do you travel to?" the lady asks.

"Canada," I say.

It is with great joy that she informs me, "Well, that would not be a problem. We could get all of the documentation ready for you to take the cat with you, whenever you travel to Canada."

I look at Rustico and think of him being given a pet passport, and then I envision the horrified expression of Canada Customs when this half-mangled cat proudly, but lamely, prances into the country and then, for an encore, goes into a coughing and sneezing fit.

"No, that really is not a consideration," I say, trying not to sound dumbfounded.

"Oh, don't worry," the ever-helpful cat lover says cheerfully. "It wouldn't be a problem at all to get the paperwork done for him. We do it all the time."

Wow, the one and probably only time in Italy that getting paperwork and documentation would not be a nightmare! I recall the frightful time David and I had getting proper documents for *me* and the bureaucratic hurdles we had to jump, but not so for Rustico!

"No, really, it is not something we can consider," I say, firmer this time.

She does not respond for a long while, and I detect that she is disappointed we didn't accept her offer of traveling abroad with Rustico.

The silence continues for what seems like an eternity, followed by a loud, deep sigh. "Well, then you must take the cat to the vet, and if the vet approves, Rustico will be taken to Gloria's house." Another long pause, then to guilt me she adds, "She already has twelve cats, but if you cannot look after even this one cat, she will take him in for you."

"I'm really sorry. We tried our best to help, but we really cannot take him in. With the traveling, he would not get the care and love he deserves," I say, trying to sound sympathetic.

Her tone changes. "Well, once the vet determines Rustico can go to Gloria's, then we will call you with her address. She lives in the countryside, and we can make arrangements for you to visit Rustico as often as you like."

I almost fall over. The cat barely lets us near him and has no particular attachment to us, unless he is demanding gourmet cat food. I picture us driving an hour through hilly country terrain to visit Rustico at Gloria's house.

I'm at a loss for words. "Okay" is all I manage to say.

The earliest appointment the vet has is a week later. We care for Rustico as best as we can during this period and spend small fortunes on gourmet cat food and prescription medication.

The day arrives to take Rustico to the vet. I am suddenly overcome by emotion for this poor animal. David puts him in his cage and places it in the car. I take one last look at Rustico and begin to cry. I hope he will be going to Gloria's, but to find out would also mean having to possibly accept the alternative. I tell David I don't want to know the truth, and I will imagine Rustico happily living away the remainder of his life at Gloria's country home in the Tuscan hills.

Hopefully, Gloria serves gourmet cat food.

Chapter 12

"Mother Sitting"

Our last guest, Rustico, has departed (no pun intended). My sister Vesna should be arriving soon, and I look forward to many a day spent relaxing and catching up. She's employed at the investment firm where I used to work and for the same high-strung broker, thus some rest is definitely in order.

But Vesna has other plans. "Could some friends drop by for a few days while I'm there?"

I have lived in Tuscany long enough to know that words like *some* and *few* are never to be taken at face value.

"They don't want to inconvenience you, so maybe they could lease Eric's rental property nearby," she says, then quickly adds, "They would also rent their own car. You would hardly notice them."

She recalls my stories of slaving over guests after a long day of driving them across vast distances of Tuscany. Although I love doing it, I do not have the stamina of an eighty-year-old Italian woman. Yet these guests are mutual friends we have known for years and can be quite entertaining. Vesna is also incredibly kind and helps both of my parents back in Canada, while I live "the high life" in Italy, so how can I not grant her this request?

Besides, how can we object, since we will "hardly notice them"?

My sister arrives, exhausted. A combination of jet lag and extreme fatigue renders her bedridden for the next several days. She sleeps till noon and consequently stays up until the wee hours of the morning. While she sleeps, I spend the day cleaning Eric's vacation home, Tillia. He purchased the stone home in a state of near ruin several years ago. He labored tirelessly restoring it, with several crews of men he brought with him from Belgium, over countless liters of wine and kilos of Tuscan steak. Considering the amount of wine consumed, the fact that the walls are straight is nothing short of a miracle. The original massive wooden ceiling beams were left in place, but new terra-cotta floors were laid, along with an addition full of windows that look out onto the green valley and hillsides covered in olive groves. The mix of old and new is perfect, with the painted furniture and the natural wood complementing each other. The once dark, sad house has been transformed and is now bright and cheerful, thanks to a dozen inebriated Belgians. There is a pool with expansive views of the vineyard. The guests should be very comfortable here.

I lug linens over, as the rental does not supply them, because most vacationers come from Belgium with their own. I provide basic grocery items, ensuring that the guests I "will hardly notice" will be self-sufficient until they get settled in. Regardless, for their first evening here, we invite them over for dinner.

Vesna cannot shake the jet lag, thus I'm surprised when she suggests taking the early train to Florence the next day.

"Florence? Why don't we wait until you're awake to see Florence?" I ask.

"Well, I'm not really going for me," she says. "We would be doing a bit of 'mother sitting.'"

I cannot wait to find out how she defines "mother sitting."

"Soja is on vacation, visiting her family in Korea. She will fly into Florence tomorrow, but her son will arrive the day after. She's seventy-five, and it's her first trip to Italy, so I promised Jason I would look after his mother for the day."

Hence, we are on the early train to Florence to "mother sit." Vesna is so dead-tired, she is barely able to sit upright. I envision a day spent trying to keep two people awake.

We enter a small building in the center of Florence, where one floor has been converted into hotel rooms. There is a desk in the middle of a hallway. We ask the "receptionist," whom I suspect is also the owner, the cleaning lady, the cook, and the security guard, for Soja. The woman also proves to be an expert spy, for she informs us that Soja is still sleeping.

We join the throngs of well-dressed Italians having their breakfast at a bar. We elbow our way to the counter, savor our cappuccinos, and return to the hotel. The receptionist informs us that "the Korean lady" is up and that she has had her breakfast. Then she asks, "Who may I say is calling?"

She walks down the hall and knocks on the door to let Soja know we are here. The receptionist has fallen short on her spying skills, though, because we discover that Soja has gone back to sleep. The woman bangs on the door, harder this time, no doubt waking all other guests, and Soja emerges, half-asleep. She is a tall, thin lady with an elegant bouffant hairstyle and is wearing a very pretty fifties-style dress. She greets my sister and introduces herself to me, while I marvel at the power of her hairspray. She has a real flair for fashion and apparently believes that elegance takes precedence over comfort, as she puts on a pair of chic high heels to match her dress.

Still drowsy, she prances out of the hotel, informing the receptionist at what hour she plans to return. I watch her with a bemused smile. If ever they were to remake *Breakfast at Tiffany's* and wanted to cast a seventy-five-year-old Korean Holly Golightly, Soja would get the part. Mother sitting may prove to be fun after all.

Soja quickly discovers that cobblestones are not that charming when one must totter across them in high heels. Every so often, she trips, giving onlookers the impression that "Breakfast in Florence" might have included a martini or two. Vesna grabs hold of one of her arms, while I carry her large, fashionable handbag. In between being a porter, I am also enlisted as a photographer—every few yards she stops and poses, gesturing for me to take another shot.

In Piazza della Signoria, we run into a young Italian man from our town. I introduce him to Soja, who, much to my surprise, asks him, "Are all Italian boys this handsome?" He shyly smiles and shrugs his shoulders. She further probes into his personal affairs by asking his age and marital status and then runs through a mental rolodex to see if she knows anyone back in Canada whom she could set him up with. She describes each prospective candidate, then shakes her head, as none will do. The single ones are either too fat, too old, or the wrong race for him. So as not to leave him feeling rejected, she adds, "If I were younger, I would marry you!"

Luca, quite taken by this eccentric older lady, suggests we meet him after work for a drink. I don't want to discover what she may be like if she actually *has* a drink, and, besides, we have a lot to see and at our current pace will need all day if we are to take in even the basic highlights of Florence. Thus, we graciously decline.

She warmly hugs Luca and waves goodbye, as we leave him standing in the square, slightly dumbfounded.

While we're en route to the charming Ponte Vecchio, vendors implore us to buy the type of souvenir that anyone under eighty would dread receiving. We wait patiently, while Soja lingers at each booth, inciting a monologue of bartering. "Okay, I'll give it to you for ten, seven, five, three . . ." Just before they pay her to take the item away, she says, "No, thanks," and off we go.

She stops to admire the handbags. The bartering monologue starts. Soja is quiet, shakes her head, and waits. Finally, the Indian man has talked himself down sufficiently, so Soja stops him. "Fine, I'll buy it."

He places the oversized purse into a shopping bag and hands it to Soja, who hands it to me.

"My son is going to kill me," she says, giggling. "I bought so much stuff in Korea that I need to buy another suitcase!"

The sun shines, heating up the stones of Florence. Soja, already tired when we picked her up, is getting more exhausted by the minute. Vesna grasps one of her arms, while I hold the other, along with the many purses that have been entrusted to my care. We look for someplace to sit down and have a coffee. We leave the main piazza and head into a small alley, where I assume everything will be less expensive.

We enter a bar and seat ourselves. We wait to be served. Then we wait some more. The people behind the counter regard us with manifest indifference. I help myself to a menu, and, on opening it, I must have exhibited visible signs of distress, for Soja quickly says, "Don't worry, I'm paying."

She doesn't appear bothered by the exorbitant prices and is happy to be sitting in an air-conditioned room. She removes her shoes from her swollen, blistered feet. Perhaps that is why we still see no sign of a waiter.

I refuse to let anyone in my care be ignored if she is willing to part with large sums of money, so I suggest we leave.

"Please hand me my purse," Soja says. I give her the bag I had been lugging, and she pulls out another pair of shoes, these ones far more sensible. She switches shoes and says, "Okay, we can go."

I take her handbag with the steaming shoes in it.

We return to Piazza della Signoria, because if we're going to pay a ridiculous amount of money for a coffee, it might as well be in the main square, dripping with atmosphere.

A handsome young waiter, formally dressed, cordially greets us and seats us next to a machine blowing mist to cool us down.

"Now this is more like it," I say. I open the menu and get a true lesson in the meaning of exorbitant. The price of a coffee is double that of the previous establishment, where I'd ordered everyone to leave, due to its steep prices.

The waiter returns, and Soja insists we order coffee and cake. Vesna and I cannot bring ourselves to, so we each order a cappuccino and will nurture it slowly to ensure that Soja gets her money's worth. We sit in the piazza and watch the handsome and not so handsome world go by, as I try not to think about the bill that will inevitably be placed on our table.

Luca had recommended a local place for lunch called Buongustai. I am keen on finding it, because Luca said the prices are reasonable and the food is good. Soja is still having difficulty walking and is far more interested in finding any place nearby, regardless of price. Vesna slowly walks with Soja, while I run ahead, loaded down with bags, to scout out menus, while hoping to find Buongustai. I finally see it and wave the girls on.

The kitchen is visible from the front window, and the small place is packed. Locals line up to take food out. The hard wooden stools without backs do not induce leisurely lingering, so perhaps we will get a table quickly. We do. They seat us at a table for four, with a single man there heartily devouring his meal. Vesna and I hunch over, while Soja sits perfectly upright across from the man. She has a regal air and arouses the interest of those around her. The elderly man at our table regularly glances in her direction.

The waitress hurriedly comes over to ask what we would like to drink. Soja launches into an elaborate explanation of how she would love a glass of wine, but her son would not allow it. I'm not sure whether it's because she's taking medication or if her son wants to spare the masses her embarrassing interrogations. Either way, because we are "mother sitting," I suggest that she obey her son. She pretends to be displeased, then orders water and returns to her smiling self. She divulges many a family secret, thus perhaps it's best she didn't have any wine after all.

We enjoy a tasty lunch from the daily menu: I order tripe in tomato sauce, and Vesna has crepes with *bresaola*, Brie, and pine nuts. Soja especially enjoys a scrumptious tiramisu. The bill, too, is very pleasing.

We show Soja a few more sights, and when she starts to display far more interest in benches than in the Duomo, we realize it's time to take her back to the hotel.

We head home on the next train. "Mother sitting," though amusing, is also tiring. Thankfully, tomorrow will be her son's turn.

Chapter 13

Tuscany, according to "the Experts"

Vesna, David, and I are lounging by the pool at Eric's holiday rental, enjoying what may be one of the last pool-worthy days of fall. I lie in a deck chair, soaking in views of olive groves, vineyards, and cypress trees on undulating hills across the valley. The sun shines and the village is still, as everyone takes a *pausa*. Even the usual roar of tractors is not to be heard. We live in paradise. I smile, feeling at peace with the world.

Vesna and David are sleeping, and I'm about to nod off when my cell phone rings.

Many people complain when guests show up late. Yet there are worse things, such as guests who show up several hours early. It is Glen.

"Hey, Jason and I picked up Soja and have left Florence and are on our way. I think we're close to your town."

Although Vesna had said, "You will hardly notice them," I begin to have my doubts. Vesna smiles meekly but remains silent.

We head back home to prepare dinner, and soon we hear their car pull into the driveway.

David gives them a tour around the vast grounds, and they are impressed. Jason's first words to me are "If you ever feel down, think about the almost eight billion people who don't live as well as you do."

I take this to mean that he loves the place. Looking around, I have to agree with him.

I have prepared several Tuscan specialties and am eager to share them, for Jason and Glen are into cuisine and, in general, the finer things of life. They have taken a cooking class in Florence today, and it won't be long before I realize how dangerous this will be for me.

I explain the antipasto, as Glen takes over and describes it for me—according to Jamie Oliver, of course.

The next course I serve is *Arista Toscana* (Tuscan pork roast) and potatoes sprinkled with fennel pollen. Glen delivers a long explanation of its ingredients and how best to prepare it, although this time it's according to Mario Batali. When I suggest a different method of preparation, based on recipes given to me by my Tuscan neighbors, Glen is dubious of my sources and tweets Mario to dispute the accuracy of my information.

It soon becomes evident they have come to let *us* know what the Tuscan experience is *really* all about.

David is not spared, as he pours the wine from the decanter, and Jason shares his extensive knowledge of Tuscan wines. As they sniff and discuss bouquets and aromas and use expressions normally reserved for fine wines, David gives me a look with a raised eyebrow. We try not to burst out laughing, for we have not served a Brunello or a Vino Nobile but rather a local "wine on tap," costing little more than a euro a liter.

Glen rudely interrupts *himself* every few minutes, as he checks to see whether Mario has tweeted him back. So far, no tweets. Glen is disappointed; my schooling will have to wait.

Finally, a tweet. Glen is thrilled, while I am stunned that one of these famous chefs is responding to him. Glen's face droops as he reads: it's his cousin, asking what time Glen wants to be picked up at the airport.

After dessert, David serves two types of grappa to these self-proclaimed "connoisseurs." One grappa is a famous, relatively pricey one, and the other is homemade by David's father, using a "secret recipe." I await the look on their faces when they drink it and, with a wicked smile, David lets them in on the "secret recipe" that includes panty hose and mint candies. At last, a technique they cannot tweet Mario or Jamie about for further clarification!

It is well after midnight, and thankfully, poor Soja, who has not had anything alcoholic to drink, is falling over. The boys reluctantly take this exhausted elderly lady home. I show them the house and the provisions I have left. I also point out the "bread bag" and explain that a baker brings fresh bread and pastries each morning to the village. If they leave the bag hanging on the hook outside with a note and funds, he will deliver fresh baked goods, usually by eight-thirty in the morning.

I bid them good night and wish them a nice stay in Tuscany.

Chapter 14

The "Hardly Noticeable" Guestapos

After a late evening, Vesna, David, and I are still sleeping when I hear a knock early in the morning. Assuming there must be a problem over at the vacation rental, I urge David to look into it. I turn over and am ready to fall back asleep when I hear, "So, where are the girls?" Soon, more voices join in. Still thinking they've come to ask about the house, I turn back over and close my eyes. More knocking, this time on our bedroom door.

"They're here for breakfast," says David.

"What? I left them breakfast at their house," I say.

David shrugs. "They've brought fresh pastries and given me their coffee orders. So you'd better wake your sister up."

I reluctantly get out of bed and wake Vesna, informing her that the guests I would "hardly notice" are here. With even more reluctance, she gets up.

And so the only travelers, probably in the history of mankind, unaffected by jet lag are in the kitchen, cheerfully enjoying breakfast. Soja's hair is perfect, and she is wearing another pretty dress, purchased in Korea.

Glen is no less exuberant in the morning, as he informs me that he thought it "would be easier to come here for coffee than making it at home."

Meanwhile, Vesna and I, disheveled, sit like zombies nurturing our *caffè lattes*.

The hard straw chairs in our kitchen must be highly comfortable, because no one attempts to leave. The morning passes, and I start making lunch.

Jason comes over, perhaps to inspect and consequently offer advice. "So what are you cooking?"

I tell him what's on the menu, and he is delighted. "I love risotto!"

I'm not sure whether that means they're staying for the midday meal, but I try to adopt the Italian philosophy of "the more, the merrier," when dealing with food and guests. I double up on the ingredients, just in case.

David pulls out maps and offers suggestions on places they could visit while they are in Tuscany. Their lack of motivation to go anywhere makes us realize that they are not here so much to visit Tuscany but rather to visit *us*. Resigned to my fate, I take this as a compliment and invite them for lunch.

The risotto turns out quite well and with "a few adjustments would really be perfect," I learn. This time there is no need to tweet Mario or Jamie, because Glen knows precisely what recommendations to make—much to the relief of Mario and Jamie, I imagine.

David serves them more of our local wine, a simple table red, not bad but not the best year for this winery. This inspires Jason to go to the supermarket to get us some really good bottles of wine. Soja, not wanting to miss a possible shopping opportunity, is eager to go, and Glen tags along, if somewhat grudgingly.

I take a long *pausa*, quite certain I will need all of my energy to make dinner for the guests I will scarcely notice.

Chapter 15

Captivating Castle

Chiara calls to invite us to lunch at her castle on Sunday. I decline, explaining, "We have guests visiting."

Chiara, with the typical Italian philosophy of "the more, the merrier," insists, "Bring them, too!"

What's a few more for lunch at a castle? I'm thrilled, because I've been curious ever since we spotted a very large key at her house and discovered it was for their castle. This castle, on a hill outside of Arezzo, is named after the village where it is located, Batifolle. The name, literally translated, means "where the crowds are fighting"—so-called, because of an old rivalry between Florence and Siena, whose areas bordered the fields of the castle. Due to its physical position, depending on who was the winner of the latest fight, it passed from the property of Florence to the property of Siena, demonstrating who had domination of that area.

The castle is also known as Castello di Totò. Totò, the celebrated comedian of Italian stage and screen, was the illegitimate child of a nobleman in one of the poorest and now most dangerous neighborhoods in Naples. As a child, he enlisted in the army simply to eat three square meals a day. He used to play drama in the street and in the small theater, to provide for himself and his poor mum. Later, his success in show business brought him riches he'd never dreamed of, plus adventures in love and jealousy. After he achieved fame from his work as an actor, a marquis adopted him, finally giving him his noble title. During his life, he had one official mate but many love affairs, one of these with a marquise. He bought the castle for her in the 1940s and spent all of his summers there, until he passed away at the age of sixty-nine. Even in death, he was unique—due to overwhelming popular demand, three funeral services were held: the first in Rome; a second in his birth city, Naples; and a few days later, a third one by the local Camorra mob boss, when an empty casket was carried along the packed streets of the popular Rione Sanità quarter, where he was born. Totò's birth home has recently been opened to the public as a museum, and fans frequently visit his tombstone. Some of them pray to him for help, as if he were a saint.

With an enigmatic smile, I casually invite the boys and Soja to the castle, as if lunch in castles of famous people is just what we do in Tuscany. I can imagine the tweets today!

We meet in Arezzo and join the convoy of cars. We park at the bottom of the hill, with Chiara's car being the only four-by-four, able to tackle the gravel road leading up to the castle. The castle, in a magnificent position, dates back to the thirteenth century. This fortification is complete with an internal courtyard, a central tower, and a small chapel.

We enter into the delightful Old World setting. High ceilings, charming frescoed walls, and an impressive fireplace adorn the massive room. A long table has been set for twenty, with a red-and-white-checkered tablecloth, candles, and a feast for forty. It is truly enchanting.

Glen and Jason nod in approval, and I pretend this is just another day under the Tuscan sun.

Chiara runs back and forth from the servants' kitchen adjacent to the grand room and continues to bring out more dishes. Lunch consists of *panzanella* salad (a tomato and bread salad, invented to make use of stale bread); a platter of cold cuts, including prosciutto; Tuscan sausage with fennel; and wild boar sausage. An assortment of pecorino cheese, peppers stuffed with tuna, and unsalted Tuscan bread and olive oil from the thousands of trees surrounding the castle is served with lunch. Chiara is a sommelier, but that does not stop Jason from debating what constitutes a Super Tuscan.

We eat for all of Italy. After lunch, Chiara takes us on a never-ending tour of the premises, as we walk through room after room, in wing after wing. Her family plans to restore it, but at the moment things are at a standstill. With so much history, each wall has to be examined prior to restoration, to ensure that no valuable frescoes are damaged and that the ancient patina is preserved. I ask Chiara several questions, fearing that Jason or Glen may answer them. We climb up steep steps to the tower and take many pictures from high above the beautiful hills of olive groves surrounding the castle.

After such a big meal and the long walk, we are ready to head home for a *pausa*. With a long succession of goodbyes, we try to exit the huge gate but discover it locked. Chiara had left the keys on the outside of the gate, and someone closed it shut, hence we are all trapped inside the mighty walls.

Trapped inside the mighty walls

I ask Chiara if there is another way out, but she laughs. "This is a castle. It is made to keep out enemies and to protect those in its walls."

The men are convinced otherwise, though, and begin to plan our escape strategy. They try to push the huge wooden door, but it will not budge. Having watched one too many Spider-Man movies, they attempt to climb the walls. Chiara smiles and reminds them these great walls cannot be climbed. After much failed planning, the "warrior men" eventually give up, recognizing that the fortified castle is living up to its name—though usually it keeps people out, not in.

Chiara calls her father, who lives a half-hour away, to come and let us out.

We start the second procession of goodbyes and kisses, because the first one has by now expired, and we eventually leave, with Glen, Jason, and Soja driving behind us. David thinks he will outsmart them by pulling into their driveway first and then saying goodnight.

He is proved wrong ten minutes later, when we hear a knock on our average-size door. At times like these, we could use our own castle.

Chapter 16

Glen and the Seven Slaves

Jason appears with several bottles of wine. I presume they have been brought in advance for the many lunches and dinners I'm expected to serve. We don't hear a peep out of Vesna—she just smiles and shrugs her shoulders. Jason has also bought us an expensive bottle of grappa, perhaps hoping to avoid further encounters with the "secret recipe" grappa. David had assured him that although pantyhose were used, he was quite certain they were clean before being inserted into his father's grappa. Yet Jason isn't taking any chances.

It's a good thing I enjoy cooking, or I might have a different attitude about our ever-present guests. I make more Tuscan specialties, and we all eat dinner together, with Mario and Jamie once again an integral part of our meal.

After dinner, Jason takes his mother home to rest and returns soon thereafter. All evening the boys and Vesna play Machiavelli, David's favorite card game, while I listen to their sinister laughter. By one o'clock in the morning, David is tired. He suggests calling it a night, but Glen protests, saying, "C'mon, we're on vacation!"

"Well, I'm *not* on vacation," I say with a parting laugh and head off to the bedroom.

I leave David to contend with Glen, and I sink into my bed, certain that in no time I will hear the now familiar knock, knock on the door, signaling that Caffé Di Felice should open for breakfast.

And so it came to pass.

Glen is full of high spirits, despite the early hour. I hear his cheerful greeting as David answers the door. I wonder what time David got to bed—

he must be more exhausted than I am.

David starts the round of coffees, and I get up. Sleeping is no longer an option with all of the noise in the kitchen. The only person who "hardly notices" the guests is Vesna, as she continues to sleep soundly.

Glen and Jason have discovered an outdoor pizza oven built into the vacation house and would like to make pizza for dinner. That cooking class in Florence has inspired them. Besides, "you know who" has a great dough recipe. It's a shame—I used to be so fond of Jamie Oliver.

I groan and say, "We've done it, and it's a lot of work and expense. I recommend you go to Roggi's in town if you want a good pizza, and it has beautiful views—"

Glen cuts me off. "The point is *making* it *yourself*, for the experience."

"I have had that experience and vowed never to do it again," I say. "After I bought all of the ingredients, it cost the same as a takeout pizza. And with takeout, you don't have to slave over a hot fire for hours. Besides, you're supposed to take Soja to Montepulciano and Pienza today."

Those who have read my first book know that I classify guests. Glen, who moments ago fell only into "the Expert" category, has now also joined the ranks of the "the Problem Solver" category, for he says, "*You* can take her tomorrow."

And what if I have other plans? I think. Yet no obstacle is too great for Glen. Recognizing defeat, I ask, "What time should we be there for dinner?"

Glen is intent on sharing the experience, however, and is like a bloodhound, the only difference being that a bloodhound would have given up by now. He insists David join him in making pizza.

David, fully aware of Glen's modus operandi, counters that although we are happy to supply wood for the oven and to bring the beer, we would never rob him of the joyful experience of preparing everything the Tuscan way.

Glen resigns himself to our party-pooping response and then places himself into a third category—the Grocery Store–Averse Guest—when he asks, "Do I need to buy Parmesan?"

They ask us to invite some friends to join us, and Glen suggests they come early. Jason and Glen go back to the vacation rental. At least, with this culinary mission they will not be coming for lunch today.

I'm outside hanging laundry when Glen runs over, frantic. "Where is David?"

"He's in the garden," I say.

"Well, I need his help." Fortuitously for Glen, a car pulls into our driveway. Friends we've have invited for the "pizza party" have arrived several hours early. Glen introduces himself and manages to convince these unsuspecting souls to assist him. Before leaving, he picks fresh basil from the garden for the pizzas. Chiara arrives and becomes Glen's latest victim.

I smile in bewilderment. Italians are very good-natured, and these ones don't seem to mind being recruited as Glen's slaves. They are so willing to lend a hand in the kitchen—a cheerful hand, at that. Something I could learn. Maybe if I live here long enough, their attitude will rub off on me.

A couple of hours later, David and I head over to see how things are faring. A table covered with dozens of ingredients has been set up near the pizza oven, and a virtual assembly line of workers prepares the pizzas. Stefano, sweltering, was commandeered to mind the blazing fire. Inside, Jason is rolling dough and covered in flour, as is the floor. Francesca and Mirko are a chopping sensation. Meanwhile, Glen sits at a table nearby, beer in hand, barking orders and mincing basil.

Our other friends, Roberta and Barbara (whom our chickens are named after), arrive, and in no time Glen also makes it possible for them to share in the pizza-making "experience."

The first few pizzas come out of the stone oven, and Glen is gratified. No doubt, he will tweet about this genuine Tuscan experience. We all taste a sample as the process continues. David and I sit at the large, rickety table under a walnut tree, facing the Val di Chio, with its stunning views of the hillsides. Soon thereafter, Glen has had enough of "the experience," and he joins us, leaving strict instructions for Stefano to keep a close eye on the fire and the pizzas. The assembly line of workers continues, without Glen, who hungrily and impatiently waits for the next batch.

Barbara and Roberta prove to be good sports, for they were around to help David and me the last time we wanted this "experience." They, too, concluded that take-out pizza was far less complicated and just as good.

Covered in tomato sauce, Vesna resembles a gunshot victim. Glen wills his slaves to work faster. Stefano, too, is bright red, as he hovers tirelessly over the wood oven, his faithful wife assisting him. Mussolini would be proud. Poor Jason, alone in the kitchen, continues to roll dough and in large part misses out on the "experience."

One by one, the workers lose steam and join us at the table. Stefano and Jason are still left standing, but barely. Hot pizzas continue to come out of the oven until no one can eat any more.

Glen is truly satisfied and feels he's proved me wrong; it was hardly any work. His "slaves," exhausted, look as if they have been in a battle and lost, but I stay silent and let Glen remain a legend in his own mind.

Vesna looks at me, smiling, and repeats her standard line of the week: "I'll make it up to you."

Glen will leave tomorrow and will drop in to say goodbye before he heads out.

I say, "Come at nine o'clock."

But he says, "Eight, will be easier."

He "reassures" us with his parting words: "Don't worry, I'll be back soon."

Bona fide evidence that Glen feels I need to improve my understanding of Italian cuisine soon arrives in our mailbox. He has sent me a book, starring none other than Mario Batali.

Chapter 17

The Old and the Restless

My mother-in-law, Maria, in her mid seventies, insists that all of these guests must have worn me out. Best we come to her house, to rest. Looking forward to a much-needed break, we're only too happy to oblige.

David packs up the car, but, despite our best efforts, we get a late start. He'll have to make up for lost time if we want to get to my in-laws' house by lunch hour. He maneuvers through our valley faster than I would like, as we start "our days of rest."

He looks at me apologetically. "If we're late, I'll have to endure my father's wrath, then an interrogation and multiple suggestions on how to arrive on time."

David is right—I've personally endured these speeches on several occasions. So, as usual, we risk life and limb in our seemingly invisible car to make our way to my in-laws', in time for the sacred ritual of lunch.

We try to make a quick stop in Norcia, located on a wide plain abutting the Sibillini Mountains. Norcia is gastronomic heaven, so most visitors come here to eat—visitors whose in-laws aren't expecting them for lunch. The area is widely known for hunting, especially of wild boar. Hence, we want to purchase the regional specialties, such as liver sausage and wild boar products, which we customarily bring to my in-laws.

With no time to spare, I should have just smiled and pointed to the sausages, but I foolishly gave the butcher my order in my thick accent.

He smiles. "So, where are you from?"

"Canada," I say, figuring a one-word answer may deter further questions.

A typical shop in Norcia

Not so. He is rather sociable and plies me with one delicious sample of salami and sausage after another, while chatting happily.

"Where in Canada are you from?"

"Toronto," I say.

"Toronto? Toronto? No, I think my cousin lives in Vancouver. They used to live . . . hmm, what was the place called?"

I list the main cities in Canada, while he concentrates, trying to remember which one.

He is not good at multitasking, for while he ponders his cousin's last known whereabouts and other details about his life in Canada, my sausages remain on the scale, un-weighed. Thankfully, David walks in, wondering where I have been.

The butcher now realizes we're in a hurry and weighs my order. He suddenly remembers he'd gotten it wrong. "My cousin used to live in Vancouver but now lives in Toronto," and, as if to reward me for being from the same city, opens my bag and throws in a couple of extra sausages at no charge.

Due to the shopping excursion taking longer than expected, we have no time to stop for coffee, and a bathroom break is out of the question, unless it's an emergency. David drives faster through the mountains than I prefer, but it seems my wrath is easier to endure than that of his father. We arrive in record time and, more important, in time for lunch.

Mama and Papa are anxious to see us after a "long absence." It has indeed been more than a month since we were last here. Giorgio smiles, as he looks at his watch.

"Good timing," he says, happy to see us, but that happiness also has much to do with the special meal that awaits, thanks to his son's arrival.

We feast as if there is no tomorrow, and after lunch, we take a long *pausa*. As I lie in bed, happily thinking that it was a good idea to come and rest, I hear Giorgio playing the accordion—the signal that *pausa* time is over.

I enter the living room and listen for a while, until I feel it's polite enough to make my exit. I walk outside and sit in a chair, facing the mountain. My plan is soon foiled, as the music suddenly becomes louder. Over the last several days, Giorgio has heard loud guitar music floating over the valley. Thus, he has decided to give this person a taste of his own medicine. Now Giorgio is outside on the terrace, playing the accordion and breaking only for dinner. Then he returns and plays on long into the night, punishing not only the culprit but us, as well as innocent neighbors.

"So, what do you think of this here?" Maria asks.

I smile, because although she asks for my opinion, if it doesn't agree with hers, she dismisses it and tries to convince me otherwise. Proof of this is everywhere: the carpet that I put in the middle of the hallway is pushed over to the far left, thus preventing anyone from walking on it. She had asked me to put away any knick-knacks I wasn't fond of, but they have miraculously vanished from the box I put them in and have nailed themselves haphazardly to the wall.

"What do *you* think of it?" is my new line.

Happy that we are "of the same opinion," Maria calls David over to hang her latest knick-knacks.

I vowed to make the best of this trip to my in-laws'. To be the perfect guest, as defined by an Italian mother-in-law, I would eat lots, sleep lots, and do everything I was commanded to do.

So I obediently take my *pausa*. With the slight breeze this evening, I accept the wool slippers and sweater Maria brought me. I let her put them on my feet and my back, as if she is a servant. I feign a deep understanding of the gravity of *la cervicale* (a stiff neck one contracts by getting "hit by air"—and even a slight breeze in the summer could leave you suffering from this mysterious Italian malady). I pretend to be grateful that she saved me from it, yet again. I resist removing the doilies on top of doilies. I act as if having six kitchen towels out and in use at once is normal, keeping in mind that one day I, too, will become old. My only indiscretion is that I refuse the extra helping of pasta that tries to make its way unsolicited onto my plate.

David's uncle Luigi has found out we are in town and has dropped in for a *caffè corretto* and to ask David to help him stack wood. *Zio* Luigi still doesn't know my name, despite us having initially lived there seven months. Regardless, *Zio* has always been so kind and helpful; thus, David willingly goes to assist.

It is 1:07 PM, and Giorgio, appearing moments away from a stroke, hangs off the balcony, staring at the curve in the road to see or hear if our car is approaching. David isn't answering his cell phone, so my mother-in-law sneaks into the living room to call *Zio*'s house to see where David is.

Giorgio gives up his post and enters the house, with a disapproving glint in his eyes. "He knows how to tell time, doesn't he?" Giorgio announces each minute that passes. "It's 1:10! It's 1:11!"

I fear for my husband. At 1:15, Giorgio sits down and begins eating alone, while cursing under his breath.

David finally arrives, sore and furious. David and *Zio,* in his mid seventies, tirelessly stacked wood, while *Zio's* grown son, who lives in the same house and is currently unemployed, watched them from the upstairs window and on occasion had the nerve to wave at them. Thankfully, this diverts Giorgio's wrath, as he now directs it at *Zio*'s son.

After the pasta, Maria places a platter full of black crispy things on the table.

Giorgio's mood changes, as he lunges at the critters and loads up his plate.

"No one makes snails as good as my wife does!" he says with enthusiasm. "Thanks to the rain, I got all these on my morning walk."

Maria, without asking, scoops a hefty portion onto my plate. I stare at the snails, and they seem to stare back. I conclude that the reason I enjoy snails in restaurants is that they neither resemble nor taste like snails. Only butter and garlic make them edible, and these snails have neither. I fill up on lots of grilled eggplant, hoping no one will notice the pile of snails left on my plate. Both Maria and Giorgio do and scrape my leftovers onto their plates.

After lunch, my mother-in-law shoos David and me to sleep like little children, whether we want to or not. When I wake up from my enforced *pausa*, I take a walk. The views are stunning, with towering mountains on one side and lights from the town of Ascoli Piceno shimmering below. And more important, according to my father-in-law, the air is good up here. After an invigorating, yet calming, walk, I return home to find the TV blaring.

View from our walk

My Canadian brother-in-law, Joe, describes Italian TV "as a cross between *Pee-Wee Herman*, the *Gong Show*, a cheesy 1980s soap opera, and an amateur talent contest, all done with 1990s technology. It's like every show is a 'spoof' of a real show. I keep waiting for the real TV to come on but . . . no."

I have to agree. Thus, Maria, David, and I sit in the kitchen, chatting, while Giorgio shushes us from the next room. We quiet down and whisper but soon forget ourselves and get into a loud, animated discussion, as Maria states that she cannot stand how Italians spoil their children. I'm unable to control my laughter at the irony, pointing out that she also spoils us. She disagrees, but the two apples she has just peeled, cut, and placed in front of me and David prove my point. Giorgio shushes us once more. We try to smother our laughter, and David suggests his father put on the wireless headphones.

Giorgio refuses and says, "But then I cannot hear what you are talking about."

There is a loud knock at the door. Uncles, aunts, and cousins enter, and Giorgio joins us. The TV continues to blare, and everyone shouts over it for hours. Giorgio pulls out the accordion. My head begins to hurt. Good thing we came here for a much-needed "rest"!

Regardless, my in-laws belong in Italy, and I'm glad they moved here from Canada. I can see they are happy. The slow, laid-back lifestyle affords them the time to garden, cook wonderful healthy meals, and visit one another, with time left over to perfect that one song on the accordion.

The next morning we head back to Tuscany, as usual with a chock-full car. David and his parents are disappointed, because we won't be able to take the choice hens they picked for us to join Barbara and Roberta. David's mom is dubious about the quality of Tuscan chickens. Either the hens or the food items had to remain, so, thankfully, it will only be me squawking all the way home.

Maria waves goodbye with tears in her eyes. I smile, knowing we will be back in no time. Italian mothers can be rather persuasive, and she really wants us to have these choice Abruzzesi hens.

Chapter 18

Earnest Ernesta

I invite Ernesta, a neighbor we have grown fond of, to our house for lunch. She insists it will prove too much for me, so instead she invites twelve of us to her house for her homemade pizza. Ernesta is ninety-three.

We arrive at 8 PM. Ernesta warmly greets us at the front door, though we could have let ourselves in, because the key is hanging on the outside.

She gives me the once-over and says, "I don't like your outfit today. I hope you are not offended by me telling you."

I'm not, but I wonder how Banana Republic is going to take it.

David gives her leeks from his garden. She also has a garden and faithfully plants vegetables every year. She digs with one hand, while holding onto her cane with the other, and has no intention of turning the job over to anyone else. Not that her grandson is remotely interested. Ernesta had not planted leeks, so she is very appreciative. David follows her to the kitchen, where she shows him her latest discovery: a round plastic "crisper" that keeps veggies "fresh."

She proudly opens the lid and says, "Look how fresh this keeps them!"

David sees the limp, discolored carrots and celery that look and feel as if they have been there far too long. He smiles and fears his leeks will share the same fate.

David hands the wine we've brought to Ernesta's son-in-law, who examines it. "Ah, a Vino Nobile, a very good wine." He nods in approval, then adds, "This wine is too good to drink tonight. I will keep it for another occasion." Thus, he breaks the Italian custom of serving wine that guests have brought.

Serving the wine that the guests have brought is a sensible Italian custom that our friend Colin, back in Canada, has recently adopted. Although certain guests enjoyed drinking Colin's expensive wine, they curiously preferred to bring cheap homemade wine. So Colin broke the Canadian custom of the host pairing the wine with the meal. He gave his guests the benefit of the doubt (though there was no doubt) and assumed they must enjoy the plonk they'd brought. Thus, he served their wine with dinner.

Ernesta's grandchildren and their children join us, along with another family. We loudly chat while the TV is on in the background, as always, featuring scantily clad Italian woman trotting around.

The older ones discuss the cost of living, and their eyes light up as they refer to prices in lire. It's amazing that they cannot comprehend fifty euro, but when referring to hundreds of thousands of lire, the value of something becomes clear. The euro was introduced in 1999, but signs in both the lira and the euro still abound.

Ernesta has made enough pizza for all of Italy.

"Ernesta, you are amazing!" I say.

"No, I'm not like I once was. I'm slowing down."

She has twelve people for dinner, her tablecloth is ironed, and she made enough pizza for a hungry soccer team. She has done all of this in a miniscule kitchen. Few from my generation could accomplish such a feat, or, if we could, it would certainly not be done without bitter complaining. Yet she is content and so happy to share.

"No, I'm really slowing down. I wanted to color my hair today but ran out of time. I cannot imagine myself with white hair," she says. The rest of us can, as we usually see three inches of regrowth before she colors it herself jet black.

"Plus, I ran out of flour and had to go to the store. No one was home to give me a ride, so I called Rosa to come and get me."

"In her *ape*?" I ask, shocked. For Rosa, also an elderly lady, drives a yellow *ape*.

"Yes. It was not easy to get in, because the passenger side door is broken, so I had to crawl in across the driver's side."

Trying not to giggle, I picture Ernesta, a hefty woman, dragging herself across the front seat, butt first, then Rosa climbing in next to her, with the two of them squished between the doors and driving through the streets of Castiglion Fiorentino at a snail's pace.

Ernesta is still slightly traumatized and continues with her explanation. "The passenger door was tied with a string, so it kept opening. I tried to hold onto the string but was worried I would fall out. Next time, if you are not home, I am calling the Romanians upstairs for a ride," Ernesta says defiantly to her grandchildren.

The family has forbidden her to ask the Romanian tenants upstairs for any more rides, because their mode of transport is a motorcycle. One day her grandchildren came home to find Ernesta on the back of the motorcycle and were alarmed. But Ernesta insists it's far safer than riding in the *ape* today. I have seen Rosa drive, and I couldn't agree more.

"Life was easier when my husband was alive." She has been a widow for many years, and a picture of her deceased husband hangs from a locket on her gold necklace. She opens it to show me, and tears well up. She loved him and greatly misses him. It is not easy living alone. She has had offers from her children to come and live with them, but she prefers to stay where she is.

I tell David that if I die, I'd like him to get one of those necklaces and to wear it always, despite the objections of his next wife. "Promise me, David?"

Not entirely certain I'm joking, he reassures me, "Mine will be twice her size."

An eighty-two-year-old guest, Cosetta, sums up her interpretation of marriage, as she says, "I'm not old, but I'm not getting remarried. What for? To wash someone else's underwear?"

Ernesta offers David the wine her son-in-law has put out. David picks up the bottle and is oblivious to the warning signals from the grandchildren. They wave, wince, and make a gagging gesture, but David doesn't notice as he pours himself a hearty glass.

He is about to swallow when Ernesta says, "I have to admit this batch is not very good. The barrel may not have been cleaned properly, as I found some bees or flies in it, not sure what they were, but don't worry I took them out, but still it's not very good this year." Regardless, she downs another gulp.

She waits for David's opinion of the wine, as he now with great apprehension puts the glass to his mouth. The grandchildren look away, fearful of the coming reaction. Dave braces himself, takes a small sip, and declares, "Let's just say the flies add a certain unique bouquet."

Ernesta laughs, strongly concurs, and has another big gulp. She changes the subject, for which David is grateful, and he puts down the full glass, hoping she won't notice. She remarks on how good her son-in-law's mother looked. "I thought she looked great."

Roberta, shocked, says, "What do you mean, she looked great? She's dead!"

"Well, she was very nicely dressed. To me, she looked better than she has in years!" Ernesta says, defending her opinion. Her son-in-law, meanwhile, doesn't seem to mind and agrees that his mother looked quite good for her age, even in the coffin, at ninety-five.

David and I are shocked, while everyone else pays no mind and gorges on pizza—except Ernesta.

"Aren't you hungry?" I ask.

"No," says Ernesta, "for dinner I usually eat light."

Roberta jumps in. "Light? She makes herself an *orzo* [barley] coffee, then pours red wine in and adds a huge tablespoon of butter." She chastises Ernesta on the detrimental effects of eating such a meal for so many years.

Though it sounds like the least appetizing concoction I've ever heard of, I don't know if it could be argued that it's not healthy, because Ernesta is ninety-three, still plants a vegetable garden, and made pizza for a dozen of us. I may just get the exact recipe.

She insists we eat until we can no more. I swear I will never be hungry again. She is from the generation that gave and never stopped giving. Perhaps that's the real secret to happiness, after all. Her broad smile tells me it is.

The custom in Italy is that guests bring dessert, thus I have made a confetti cream torte. I cut Ernesta a large piece, and she quickly polishes it off. Cosetta insists I give Ernesta another hefty piece, despite Ernesta's protests. I don't know who to obey, so I cut another slice and give it to Ernesta, who finishes it pronto.

Limoncello is served after dinner. Ernesta swears, "It is full of vitamins and should be drank every day."

Who can argue with her?

Cosetta lives up the street and a few years ago returned to Tuscany. "I went down to Naples to help my son with his Laundromat for a few days and stayed for twenty years. I kept meaning to come back but never did. In the end, a man comes into the Laundromat and complains about a stain on his shirt. He kept pointing to this stain that I could not see, so I flipped. The next day I packed my bags and left. I've been grateful to that man ever since."

Ernesta insists on packing cookies for us for breakfast. She drops a few on the floor, surveys them and then us, and gives us clean ones, while placing the others back onto the pile. While not entirely approving of this maneuver, I do appreciate this generation and their disdain for waste.

We vow to keep this our secret. On occasions like these, ignorance is bliss.

Chapter 19

Olive, Our Love

It is late fall. A thick fog encompasses the valley each morning. The days get shorter, and the sun pokes through only occasionally. Hunters and their dogs freely roam our fields, and we regularly hear gunshots. The village turns even sleepier. The smell of grapes permeates the air, as trucks drive by with their harvest. The vines turn golden yellow and orange on the hillsides, and pomegranates weigh down their branches, while persimmons hang on trees like ornaments. Seasons have meaning, and anticipation for what each one brings makes the wait worthwhile. Many happy moments are in store for us: the festival of porcini mushrooms, the festival of truffles, and the festival of the wild boar.

Invites to taste new wine and roasted chestnuts abound. And, best of all, I only need to iron the fronts of David's shirts until springtime.

Enzo, our neighbor, drops in with a *schiacciata con l'uva*, a typical Tuscan focaccia studded with grapes during the wine harvest. When we first met him, he enthusiastically told us he would soon retire and would finally have time for his hobby.

"What is your hobby?" we asked.

"Please don't laugh, but I love cooking."

We almost laughed out loud, simply because he'd asked us not to. Small-village life had obviously taken its toll on him. With great eagerness, he talked about food and the fresh ingredients he uses from his vast garden. He insisted that as soon as he is retired, he will make us an authentic Tuscan meal.

"Then we, too, eagerly await your retirement!" we both said.

The next day he invited us over to show us his gardens, both vegetable and flower. His wife, Giovanna, also loves gardening, and she has built a long stone wall terrace, in which she planted the largest herb garden imaginable, with scents of lavender, mint, rosemary, and lemon balm. The rosemary is prolific, a deep green with delicate purple flowers in full bloom. She also had artichokes mixed in with this medley of herbs for the sheer beauty of their flowers—though she is quick to tell us that she "must always keep an eye on them, for I have caught my father-in-law trying to take them."

I am dubious about the fate of the artichokes. Letting them go to waste may be more temptation than the old man can bear. Afterward, we enjoyed drinks and have since remained the best of friends.

The intermittent rain is foiling Enzo's plans to pick olives and take them to the mill. If he doesn't pick the remaining olives soon, the ones he has already collected may get moldy.

We offer to help the next time the weather permits.

The next day the sun is shining brightly, and Enzo, though normally reserved, calls to take us up on our offer.

We walk the few minutes to his house, and Enzo is outside, laying down nets under a row of trees, one on either side of the tree trunks, making sure to secure the nets along the center. Giovanna, meanwhile, prefers to pick by hand and has a basket strapped around her waist.

David picking olives

Giovanna's preferred method of picking olives

Enzo is wearing black rubber boots, a thick winter jacket, and a toque, while Giovanna is dressed to match. David and I, the resistant Canadians, don far lighter clothes.

I pick the olives with a tool that resembles a child's sandbox rake. I comb the olives off the lower branches and onto the nets. Enzo and David, meanwhile, pull the olives down off the branches with their bare hands.

Once the olives have been picked and dropped onto the net below, we gather the nets and roll the olives into piles and remove any branches and large leaves. David and Enzo then lift the nets and carefully load the olives into plastic crates.

Enzo loves the tradition of growing his own olives and pressing them for oil. Antonio, Enzo's eighty-five-year-old father, tends a grove across the valley.

Giovanna and I chat while picking, while Matta, their adorable cat, happily plays among us. This is all so novel and enjoyable for the first few hours, but soon I have a newfound appreciation for farm work and will never look at another bottle of olive oil the same. Thus, to my great relief, Enzo announces lunchtime.

We enter the massive addition they have built onto their stone house, attached to his father's house. Enzo has moved a total of fifteen feet his entire life. Giovanna is enthralled with all things ancient, and the floors are reclaimed terra-cotta tiles, costing far more than new ones. The kitchen cabinets are made of reclaimed wood. A built-in cabinet has two doors, one with a pane of glass, while the other is boarded up with wood—because this was the economical solution in the past when glass broke.

A feast awaits us, with a platter of Tuscan meats, an assortment of pecorino cheeses, and a sage-and-olive-oil focaccia, freshly made by his aunt. Lunch would not be complete without a bowl of hot pasta, so Enzo serves us penne in his famous *ragù* sauce. Unlike picking olives at a hurried pace, lunch, including espresso and homemade *crostata* ("jam tart"), is savored leisurely.

Back to work and back to having even more respect for farmers. We labor until it's almost dark, and Enzo declares it a job well done. He insists we stay for dinner. We protest, because he, too, must be exhausted, but he is adamant, saying, *"Non si invecchia a tavola"* ("One does not age at the table").

And so we are rewarded with a dinner of Tuscan steak with shaved truffle on top, fine wine, and friendship. Enzo loves to experiment and has produced a variety of grappas and flavored liqueurs.

We astonish them by saying, "It's against the law to make spirits yourself in Canada."

They conclude that Canada is not the Promised Land, after all.

We help Enzo pick several more days until every last olive is off the trees. He has an appointment at the local mill, which uses a cold-press method to preserve the quality of the olive oil. The press currently runs twenty-four hours a day.

At the mill, Enzo warmly greets the owner. The olives are first weighed, then put into a funnel, and a steel lattice overlay helps catch any leaves and branches as the olives tumble down. The olives travel along a conveyor belt to remove any stray leaves. Enzo moves along with them, never taking his eye off his batch of olives. Other farmers do the same. Once the leaves are removed, the olives are washed with cold water. Next, the olives are pulverized under two large revolving stone mills. The crushed paste is moved into a large centrifuge that separates the oil from the paste. The oil goes to a smaller centrifuge, where it is refined further. The oil is then strained and filtered, and soon the green gold drizzles out into the steel vat Enzo holds under the spout. He is like a proud father.

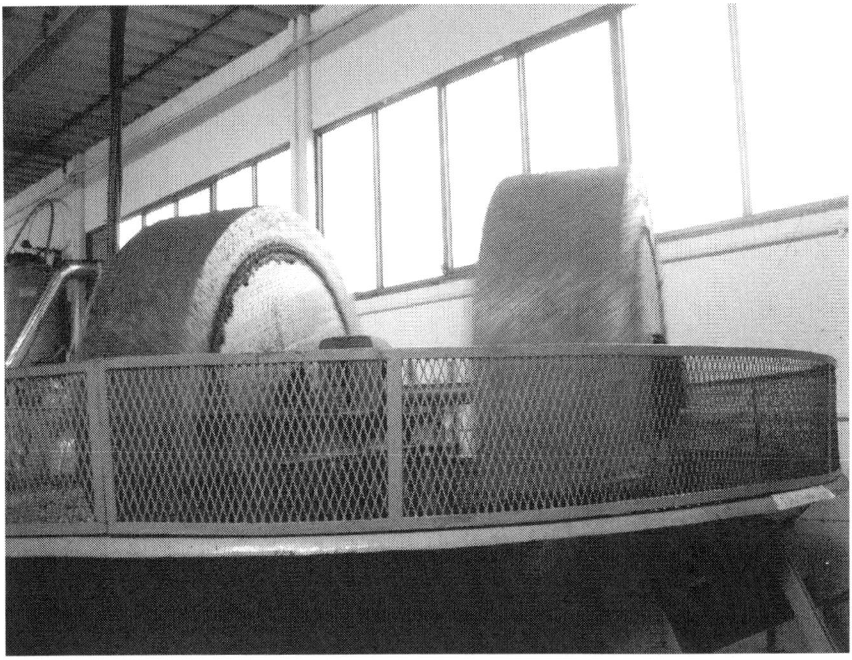

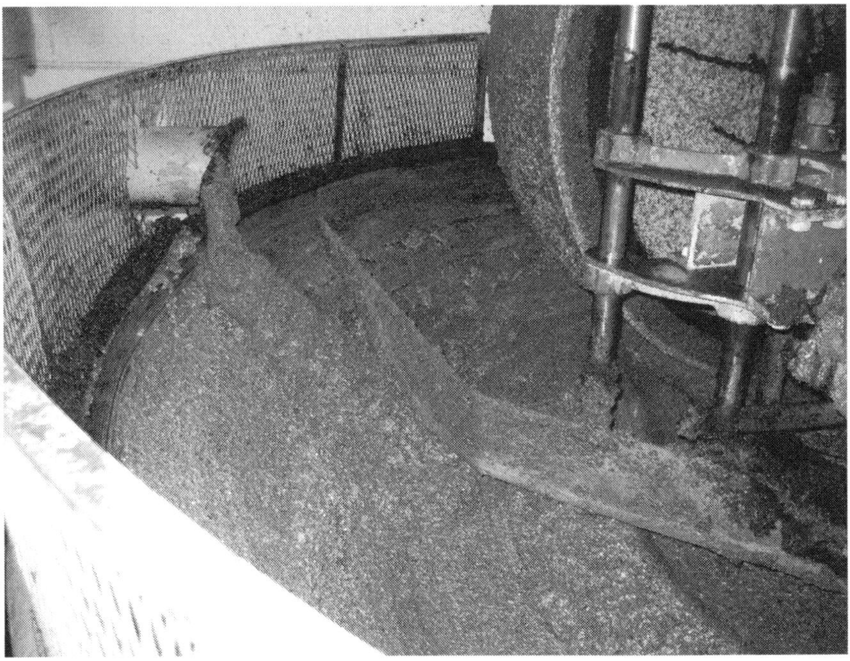

Enzo will remain as the oil drizzles out slowly. David and I head home, having had enough of the experience to know that no matter what the price is this year, it will be worth every euro cent.

Liquid gold

The following day, Enzo arrives with a liter and half of neon-green olive oil. For weeks, we devour Tuscan bread heavily drizzled with the new oil and sprinkled with salt. Fall has brought memorable moments, some more lasting than others, including the five pounds we have each gained.

Chapter 20

Four Saps in a Tub

I am "sinfully" sipping a large American coffee when I hear a lot of fanfare outside. I do a double take, because an army vehicle appears to be chugging away in our driveway. Eric, the man whose two rental properties we care for, has arrived with his friend Philippe.

We had met Philippe on one of Eric's self-proclaimed "work/dream vacations." Though a plumber by trade, Philippe loves to cook and was enlisted to do both on his trips with Eric. Eric can be rather convincing, and no doubt he wins most of his cases as a lawyer. He found Philippe under "Plumbers" in the phone book.

Eric starts with intrigue. "Hello, my name is Eric. I'm a lawyer, and I have a proposal."

Immediately after hearing Eric's proposal, Philippe concluded that this was a scam by a travel agency—and not a very clever one, because he could see right through it. But Eric is very persuasive and in no time was sitting in Philippe's living room.

Eric used his charm, along with an appeal to the victim's desire for a self-indulgent vacation that would be light on the pocketbook. "You work one day and tour Tuscany the next day, all expenses paid."

And so the poor man, who moments ago was sitting in his living room, happily chugging Belgium beer, inevitably agreed to get into a minivan with Eric and a motley crew of Belgians and drive to Tuscany for a "work/dream vacation," while their astonished wives waved goodbye.

"We just arrived," says Eric. "We drove eighteen hours straight from Belgium."

Ever since we began working for him, he has been very kind to us. At the end of each stay, guests would saunter over and curiously gift us leftover food and wine, which we gratefully accepted. We later learned that Eric had put it in his rental instructions for the guests to take extra food and drinks to the "needy" couple down the street.

I presume he and Philippe are looking for a hot meal or, at the very least, a few glasses of wine to celebrate their safe arrival.

I greet them with the customary Belgian triple kiss, while staring at the two-ton monster parked outside: a Land Rover Defender. It is fifteen feet long and seven feet tall, not well suited for touring quaint hilltop towns; parking will be a nightmare. Inside are two original seats in the front and several wooden benches in the back. Seatbelts must be optional in Belgium.

"I use it to transport my horses in Belgium. My van broke down soon into the trip, so we either had to forfeit coming or take the Defender," says Eric.

Judging by their physical state, forfeiting the trip might have been the wiser choice. I imagine the vehicle swaying back and forth drunkenly as Eric drove at maximum speed, costing a fortune in gas. It's a vehicle for adventure, and any trip with Eric is always an adventure.

This is confirmed when they enter the house, accompanied by the strong smell of diesel fumes. Every so often, they double over in a coughing fit, as their lungs try to expel the exhaust toxins. Eric stands next to the woodstove to warm up, and I worry that he will combust.

We offer them wine, which they gladly accept, while I make them something to eat.

Eric has an announcement and wants our undivided attention, though he routinely wants our undivided attention.

"Madam, tomorrow I am taking you to the thermals." This is not a question but rather a statement.

I envision David and I bouncing off the benches in the back of the Defender, trying to remain upright, while Eric drives maniacally, pushing the beastlike vehicle to its limits, with adventure gleaming in his wild eyes.

Eric paces back and forth, arranging our "relaxing" day at the thermals.

"We can take our car, because you drove all the way from Belgium," I say.

"No, it will be fun to go in the Defender!" Eric insists.

Fun for whom? The two people in the front seat, as they watch the two saps in the back try to stay on the bench as if they're contestants in a bull-riding contest?

David sees the unmasked horror on my face and knows I'm already imagining going off a cliff, our bodies never to be found, my second book tragically left unfinished.

"My wife would be more comfortable in our car," David says, yet quickly adds, "But if you want to go in the Defender, we can meet you there."

Eric is defeated, something he is not accustomed to, but perhaps due to inhaling fumes for eighteen hours he shrugs his shoulders and agrees.

They devour the pasta as if they have not eaten in a week, and as the wine bottle empties, Eric's catch phrase becomes "Allo, allo! You stupid woman!" based on a British show he is fond of. David endures the brunt of Eric's newfound expression, followed by insane laughter.

This is going to be a long night . . .

Both men already looked like hell when they arrived, but as further fatigue sets in, combined with the aftereffects of too much pasta and wine, they really look the worse for wear. Philippe's long blond hair still appears wet two hours after coming in from the rain.

Thankfully, the evening comes to an end, because David has been called a "stupid woman" as many times as is humanly possible to bear.

"See you first thing in the morning," Eric says.

I wonder what "first thing in the morning" means, but judging from their current state, no alarm clocks will be necessary.

I was wrong. I am still half-asleep when I hear loud, frantic banging.

"David, someone is at the door. Who could it be?" I ask.

David checks the time, reluctantly gets out of bed, and shuffles to the front door.

"David!" says Eric. "Are you not ready? I said we would be here first thing in the morning!"

Philippe is outside in the rumbling Defender. Eric is inappropriately cheerful, given the hour, and seems miraculously well rested. "Let's go! We want to get there early!"

David, still not fully awake, agrees. "Okay, we'll be ready in a few minutes."

"Fine!" Eric says and steps inside, to ensure that David keeps his word.

The automatic espresso machine starts its loud grinding, and I get up to start my "relaxing spa day."

"Good morning, Madam!" yells Eric, as I wander through the kitchen en route to the bathroom. Loud, jovial people are terribly annoying first thing in the morning. I trudge back to the kitchen to sit slightly stunned over my mug of American coffee, when Eric gleefully says, "Okay, let's go!"

I realize we must, because we agreed to last night. "I'll need a few minutes to pack lunch."

"No need, Madam!" Eric yells. "I have brought a pot, and at the top of the hill, where the boiling water seeps out, we will cook our pasta. The mountain spring will cook for us!" He points his palms upward, like a madman.

I try not to laugh at him, but the thought of pasta boiling away at the top of the thermal mountain is surreal.

Eric sees me packing a few things, "just in case," and stops me. Semi-crazed, he says, "The mountain will cook for us!"

I pretend to obey and agree to be ready in a few minutes.

Eric goes outside to announce to Philippe that we shall be departing shortly.

"He's crazy," David says.

"He's making me crazy!" I say to David and quickly pack assorted cold cuts, bread, cheese, fruit, and water into a knapsack, hoping Eric won't notice.

David goes out to stall for time, and when I come out, the two men are sitting in the Defender, refusing to budge.

"Okay, get in," he demands.

"No, Eric," I tell him, "we said we're going to take our car."

He watches me get into our car, then shakes his head and tells Philippe, "Madam wants to take their car."

Philippe, still smelling like eau de diesel, obeys, grabs all of the wine, and climbs into the backseat of our ancient BMW. Eric, carrying a pot, a bag of pasta, and a bottle of tomato sauce, crams in next to Philippe, with a soliloquy on how we would be much better off in the Defender.

I soon agree with him. When David and I drive alone in our deafening

BMW, I wear earplugs. But doing so with other passengers would be rude, thus I endure the sensation of being in a loud jet, while trying to converse with people behind me. Eric has a lot to say, starting with his relationship with his mother. He speaks over the loud roar of the engine. He is now at age seven; only forty more years to go . . .

After an hour of driving through the stunning Val d'Orcia and after two decades of Eric's life, we see a symbol for the thermal spa Bagni di San Filippo and turn at the sign. The waters of San Filippo were known by Romans, became famous in the Middle Ages, and treated prominent people such as Lorenzo il Magnifico and other princes of the Medici family.

View en route

David searches for parking, but Eric says, "This is not where we're going. We're going to the natural spa, the free one. Keep driving."

Often, the word *free*, when associated with relaxing outings, makes me dubious, but even more so now. A little farther ahead, Eric barks, "Park here!"

David and I carry our knapsacks with towels and lunch, while Eric insists on taking the metal pot and ingredients for making pasta. Philippe lugs several liters of red wine.

We walk through the park. It is a gray, drizzly day. The forest and its murky stream do not seem remotely appealing. We spot a "DANGER—No Climbing and No Bathing" sign.

Eric says, "Follow me!" and takes off like a bullet, crossing the stream with his shoes still on. I fear getting arrested, though that may at least put an end to this escapade.

We throw caution to the wind and traipse behind him, to arrive at a fascinating formation of limestone bluffs, with individual light blue pools carved in rock at different levels. The limestone rocks are so white that at first glance they look like snow and ice.

"Come, come," Eric says, as he climbs up the perilous rocks.

We stand at a safe distance on the other side, as Eric, already down to his bathing suit, immerses himself into one of the little pools filled with hot sulfurous water.

"Aaahh," Eric says, as if filming a commercial promoting the immediate healing effects of thermal waters.

"Come, Philippe!" shouts Eric, negating any relaxing spa-like effect.

Philippe's face conveys his deep dilemma; he wishes to enter the world of hot thermal waters but is averse to leaving behind the liters of wine he is clutching. Philippe disrobes, places one bottle on the bench, and risks life and limb to carry the other bottle safely up the rock. Eric cheers him along, raunchily whistling and howling.

I put on my purple rubber-bottomed swimming shoes, and, because I am not German, by so doing announce that I have reached old age. I wade into the stream. The Spider-Man-like shoes aid in climbing the steep crevices, and soon I reach Eric and Philippe, each lying in his own little "tub" of water, drinking red wine out of a plastic cup.

I stash the knapsack full of "contraband" food in a safe place and climb down into my own personal little "tub." The waters are high in sulfur and calcium, which explains the formation of the white rocks. My body just fits, and I lie in the hot water, finally smiling as I enjoy the views and worry about going to prison. I close my eyes and begin to relax, when I sense a presence hovering over me. It is Eric.

"Madam, time to cook the pasta. Let's go to the source. Come with me!" He scurries up the hill, carrying the metal pot, a bottle of water, the bag of pasta, and tomato sauce. I reluctantly walk up the mountain with Eric. We arrive at a dilapidated pipe sticking out of the rock, with hot water abundantly flowing from it.

Eric smiles triumphantly. "See, I told you we didn't need to pack lunch."

He rigs up the pot, so that the steam will boil the water. "In twenty minutes, we will return and put the pasta in to boil."

I look at Eric and the pot and laugh to myself. I take a vow of silence, grateful I had the sense to disobey and pack a knapsack full of food.

We climb back down and find David and Philippe happily warming themselves in their individual "bathtubs." The bottle next to Philippe is almost finished, and Philippe wears a big smile.

"We shall soon eat!" Eric says. "The mountain will cook for us!"

He sees the bottle next to Philippe, and his mood changes when he discovers the bottle is just about empty. His warrior-like instinct takes over, as he climbs down the steep rocks to rescue the other bottle on the bench. I wonder when the day will end. I take solace in the "tub" made to fit my "full-figured bottom" and close my eyes to relax.

Enjoying the hot thermal waters

In no time, Eric yells, "Madam! Time for the pasta!"

I am not sure why I must accompany him but nonetheless get out of my comfortable soak and head up the rocks.

The water is hot, thus Eric puts in the package of pasta. The pasta sits in the bottom of the pot, limply. Not wanting to quell his grand ideas, I remain silent and climb down, knowing only too well that soon Eric will be shouting for me to help with lunch once again. Thankfully, the cold cuts and cheese await.

Eric's attempt at making lunch

I happily pour myself some wine from the ever-diminishing bottle and return to my welcoming hot tub, to marvel at the natural beauty of this intriguing place. I take a sip of wine and lean back, when Eric, in a fit of delirious joy, yells, "Madam! Lunch is ready."

I get out of the warm water. Eric climbs like a mountain goat, while I stagger up the hill with far less enthusiasm. The pot of pasta shares my lack of enthusiasm and refuses to boil. The penne sit in the bottom of the pot, getting soggier. Eric is perplexed but, unfortunately, still persistent. He stirs the mushy pasta and insists it needs more time, so we wait. I fear another season may be upon us before this happens, as I sit in the cold wind in my wet bathing suit.

At last, Eric decides the pasta is done. It is a soft lump of unappetizing mush, but Eric will not admit defeat. He adds the tomato sauce, and we crawl down.

Trying not to smirk, I put out the contraband food and watch the hungry men, including Eric, devour it.

In defiance, every so often he eats the pasta, which resembles something regurgitated, and insists we try it. "It's really quite good."

We abstain, knowing Eric is a lawyer and capable of embellishing whenever necessary.

After lunch, we return to our respective tubs, but when the last of the wine is consumed, Philippe suggests it is time to go home.

Basting Eric

We gather up our things and return to the car. In the close confines of the BMW, the smell of rotten eggs lingers, mixing with the reek of diesel from Eric's and Philippe's jackets.

We arrive back at the house, and Eric says, "That is how you treat your wife to a nice, relaxing day at a thermal spa."

Thankfully, David knows better than to take Eric's advice.

The men pull off their jackets and make themselves at home, so I ask, "Would anyone like pasta for dinner?"

This time, David and Philippe unhesitatingly answer, "Yes, please!"

Chapter 21

Coming to a "Grinding" Halt

Despite the "spa-like" day yesterday, we discover that Eric's reason for coming to Tuscany is less than idyllic. His house, Tillia, was finished, and he could finally relax and reap the rewards of his hard labor. But Eric always has to have something going on. With his wife's reluctant blessing, he purchased a second property, promising it would be restored without her assistance. She is a wise woman who is interested in being on vacation and understands the meaning of the word.

"The Mill" had sat vacant for years, but Eric saw this as an opportunity and snatched it up.

The documentation was erroneously completed, but despite this, Eric was the proud new owner of this home. At least, for now . . .

The restoration began. The five-hundred-year-old stone structure, formerly a mill, had inspired Eric. A lesser man would have been deterred from hauling huge pieces of ancient mills from Belgium down to Italy as mere décor, but Eric's dream would not be quashed by the logistics of transporting a few thousand tons of machinery.

Accompanying these massive pieces of mill were crews of workers from Belgium. It was at this point that David and I entered Eric's life, or, more precisely, he entered ours, for Eric always makes a grand entrance. Having gone to the employment agency and been told, "There is no work now, nor will there be any time in the future," we made up advertisements and placed them in mailboxes of homes in the area. Eric showed up on our doorstep, flyer in hand, and hired us on the spot.

"The Mill"

Now that we were part of Eric's unofficial crew, he insisted we attend an employee dinner. We walked over to Tillia, a short distance away, and joined Eric, Philippe, and a dozen Belgian men.

Miraculously, Philippe's wine glass was always full—the Belgians ensured that their cook was well cared for. Philippe's energy knew no bounds, as he ran from the BBQ, grilling and serving Tuscan steak after steak, then scurried to the porch, where Belgian fries sizzled, then off to the kitchen, where two dipping sauces for the fries boiled away—all with glass of wine in hand. The food and drink were never ending. It was not only eighty-year-old Italians we couldn't keep up with. As the evening proceeded and the wine jugs emptied, the men got louder and rowdier.

Midnight approached, and Eric demanded law and order. "My workers must get a good night's rest, because much needs to be accomplished tomorrow."

The construction crew howled in laughter. The empty jugs of wine were removed, and a variety of liqueurs replaced them. Eric was dumbfounded, for Philippe had spent the entire week's allowance for food and liquor in one day. No one paid any heed to Eric and his repeated requests for them to call it a night.

Eric said, "This is mutiny on the *Bounty*!"

The workers threatened to form a union. Admitting defeat, Eric poured himself another drink. It was late, and we were tired, thus David and I made our way home. The Belgians showed no signs of fatigue and would no doubt be up partying until the wee hours.

Despite the prolific amounts of wine consumed, the Belgians miraculously rose from the dead the next morning and cheerfully waved to us as they headed to the mill.

Not all Italians were happy that foreigners were buying up Italian homes, as was brought to Eric's attention by a cantankerous neighbor. "Do you think this is the Congo?"

Eric could not let this comment pass and in large letters painted the words BAR CONGO on the door of his pizza oven.

It was time for retribution on the part of the neighbor. He telephoned the police, alerting them to unauthorized workers. They arrived and searched the premises for these so-called illegal laborers. None were to be found, thanks to a hidden closet and a strong resolve on the part of the Belgians to huddle and forfeit breathing.

With the inspection finished and nothing found, the police bid Eric a good day.

Regardless, in a few days the mill was transformed. Construction materials were put away, and the crew celebrated with more wine, while I cleaned the property, and Eric added some final touches.

The men indulged in another evening of food and drink, with their last day of their "dream vacation" being a day of touring. I wondered how much of their holiday they would remember, judging by the countless empty gallons of wine strewn across the porch. Belgians, it appeared, were indestructible.

However, the story did not end "happily ever after."

Eric, though a lawyer in Belgium, is not a lawyer in Italy. Here there is a well-established ritual of cheating, saving money, and ripping off the government. Because paying taxes on the entire transaction price will cause certain Italians great distress, in order to alleviate this and lessen taxes, the price is "adjusted" on documents. A foreign couple we once met brought more euros in a bag to the notary's office than the amount of the check. She described the whole clandestine process, counting money for hours prior to the transaction.

Yet unbeknownst to Eric, when a property or land is up for sale, the bordering property owner has the right of first refusal at the asking rate. The person in question did not want to purchase the house or land for the going price. Yet because Eric's paperwork had erroneously been filled out, the purchase price was much lower. Suddenly, the adjoining neighbor was very interested and had the right to reclaim the land and the house for the price stated in the contract.

"I expect a bit of stealing from the Italians," Eric matter-of-factly says. "When I gave them money to buy and plant four hundred grapevines, and I only ended up with three hundred and twenty, this was to be expected. In fact, it makes me happy to know we are drinking the same wine!" He sorrowfully shakes his head at the painful memory. "But this . . . this is going too far."

We had previously not been privy to village gossip, but Eric has shattered all notions that we are part of an idyllic town.

"Don't tell this to the people who rent the house," says Eric, fearing it will ruin their vacation. "Ignorance is bliss. Let the foreigners think Italy is a paradise and that all Italians are wonderful, generous people—because, for the most part, they are."

Eric spends the next several days driving the Defender to lawyers' offices, court proceedings, and the like. I hope his skill as a lawyer proves handy.

Chapter 22

Auto Lotto

Eric has his problems, and we have ours, albeit ours are significantly smaller. Choking and coughing noises surround us daily, but this time they come from our car. The BMW 320 is showing signs of age. The fighter jet sound grows increasingly louder, and our tranquil life has become less so with each moment I spend in the car. I wear earplugs, and when friends join us, we all must yell. My phobia of high speeds worsens, because 30 miles per hour sounds like 100.

The car will cost thousands to repair. It is registered as an antique, so we pay very little yearly in insurance and *bollo* (annual car tax). Thus, it is with deep regret that David concludes it's time to say goodbye—to the car, that is.

We are not eager to begin the process of searching for a "new" car. Memories of missed appointments and prices being upped at the last moment are still vivid. We concentrate on our happy ending: the kind, generous man who gifted us the car and how well it has served us.

Due to the many steep hilltop towns, David agrees to purchase a car with an automatic transmission for me. This is for the benefit of any cars that may end up behind me on a steep hill and for all who are not hearing impaired who have to endure my peeling out. Our Italian friends distrust cars with automatic transmissions and warn us against them. Not only our friends but most people in the province of Arezzo feel this way, for few such cars are for sale. David will have to travel to the north of Italy to buy one.

We search the Internet. There is a nice man who currently happens to be in London, but if we send him the funds, he will send us the car and will give us a money-back guarantee if it is not as promised. A sweet lady who happens to be visiting sick family members in Romania has a great Mercedes for us, and if we send her the money, she, too, will ship us the car, and she fortuitously also provides a money-back guarantee. There is even a gentleman in Nigeria . . .

An eight-year-old black Mercedes C180 station wagon is for sale. The owner highlights that it is already full of scratches, as if this were a selling feature. He adds, "If you want to own a black Mercedes, you will have to get used to it. People scratch them all the time."

We no longer specify the color black when searching for a Mercedes.

At last, David finds a car in Brescia, up toward Milan, and after asking a list of pertinent questions and being given satisfying answers, David will make the long trek to Brescia. I pack him some snacks, because he will take the overnight train.

The crowded train has people sitting in the aisles, and the stale air is unbearable. David doesn't sleep the entire night and will be grateful to return home in his new car tomorrow.

Our friends Roberta and Barbara, originally from Brescia, arranged for a local mechanic to examine the car with David. They meet up with the seller in the main square, and the mechanic hops into the driver's seat, with David next to him, while the owner gets into the back.

Much to the surprise of David and the owner, the first test to be conducted is the zero to sixty, immediately followed by brake reaction times. The mechanic checks this several times, as heads fly back, then forward, which simultaneously tests everyone's neck reflexes.

Next, he accelerates like a racecar driver, leaving a huge cloud of smoke and two black lines on the pavement as an ode to power. David and the owner hold on for dear life. The mechanic is engrossed in his maniacal maneuvers and cannot stay in a lane for more than two seconds, viewing all other cars as obstacles and waiting until the last possible moment to brake before impending doom. Finally, the owner expresses his fear, so the mechanic comes to an abrupt stop. David is relieved he will live to see another day and steps out of the car.

The mechanic, with no less finesse, rips open the hood to do a visual inspection. He is not pleased and whispers his concern that the car has far more mileage than stated. The man is also missing all of the documents showing yearly maintenance that he promised he would bring. There is no deal. The "joy ride" with the crazed mechanic was for nothing.

David regrettably returns by train.

We find another BMW 320, seventeen years younger than the one we are currently driving. Once more, it is in Brescia. David, valuing life and that much wiser, sends the mechanic to inspect the car on his own. It passes all of his rigorous tests, though we don't know what condition he left the owner in. David takes the train once again to Brescia to purchase the car and pay the mechanic.

He drives home in our "new" nine-year-old car, another blue BMW 320, this time a station wagon. David honks exuberantly. I, too, am delighted. I hop into the car and revel in the quiet engine. Smiling, I say, "Now, I feel like a millionaire."

David's sister Filomena and her husband, Joe, kindly pick up our old car and drive it down to Abruzzo to David's parents, where we have found a buyer. After only a few-hour trip, they express astonishment and disbelief that we have driven this car all of these years. Apparently, Filomena's ears are still ringing.

A young Albanian boy is thrilled to buy the car. He is a mechanic, and currently his means of transportation to and from work, unbeknownst to the customers, are their cars—the ones he's working on. My in-laws take the boy in, feed him, and spend several hours getting to know him until the registration office re-opens. They help with the paperwork and finding insurance, despite the boy insisting he doesn't need any. In the end, he is grateful and waves goodbye, as he speeds off in his car that sounds like a Ferrari—which, for a kid his age, is probably a bonus.

Chapter 23

Rom-antic

After many months of fog and dreariness, spring is approaching. We haven't been to Rome in a while, and I think about how romantic it would be to visit Rome in springtime. Full of excitement, I mention this to our friends, and they are quick to agree—Rome in the springtime is very romantic, so naturally, we should all go together. Fortunately, some of them can go for only two days, thus David and I leave earlier, avoiding the long convoy that will travel together.

Despite the warmth of the season, I pack the pink wool socks and the fuzzy green pajamas David's aunt gifted to me on a previous visit. She will no doubt feel gratified as she examines my pajamas while we tour.

We arrive at our regular, if not preferred, accommodations in Rome: economics have once again dictated we stay at *Zia* and *Zio*'s place.

Zia has been expecting us, and as we enter, she gives us the once-over. "Life in Italy has been good to you. Those pale, pasty faces you had when you first arrived several years ago are gone." She surveys my buttocks, larger than before, smiling and winking in approval.

We're taken to our regular room and are briefed on all things pertaining to our lodging. The forbidden towel containing *Zio*'s germs is now blue, while the towel to wipe away *Zio*'s accidental sprinkling around the toilet is red. As if the thought had crossed my mind, *Zia* reminds us, "I cannot kill him!"

Despite the warm temperature, I am outfitted with another pair of wool socks, which *Zia* forcefully puts on top of my pantyhose, then am given slippers. Ready for the great Canadian north, we continue our tour.

Zia has been busy since our last visit and shows us a drawer full of socks she has knitted in her favorite colors, primary ones. She has also bought me a wool undershirt and an apron. Once again, I am almost the perfect poster girl for a sixty-plus *casalinga* ("housewife"). Almost, because I do not have enough cleavage.

Now we must eat, lest we perish, and as always, *Zia* has prepared enough pizza to feed a dozen, because there will be four of us. Accompanying the pizza is *Zio*'s nasty wine. There seems to be a direct correlation between the rich old men I know and their taste for dreadful wine. And *Zio* insists on generously refilling our glass after each painful sip.

We speak of life in Tuscany and how lovely it is.

"That's great!" says *Zio*. "It's always good for us to have a place to visit regularly."

I almost choke on my food (and not just on the wine), but *Zio* continues.

"I've heard they have very nice homes up there. Some even almost as nice as this one!" he proudly declares.

Keeping a poker face is no easy feat, as I look around at the assortment of cheap plastic souvenirs, the names of cities stamped on them in shining gold letters.

We discuss homes, or, more accurately, *Zio* continues his soliloquy, and we quietly learn about the superiority of Italian ones. Finally, we get a word in and talk about our house in Canada. There is confusion on his part, because he seems to think we are talking about the house in Tuscany.

Zia sets him straight, as she yells, "*Stupido*, they are not talking about their house in Tuscany, they are talking about their house in America!"

Conversation is lively and maintained throughout the meal, with at least three discussions carried out with any given individual at any given time. *Zio* keeps interrupting, even himself, and saying, *"Ascoltami"* ("Listen to me") and, despite no one listening, continues his story.

After lunch we are ushered to our room to take a *pausa*, for which I am grateful, because a combination of *Zio a*nd his wine is highly sleep-inducing.

Since our friends won't be joining us until tomorrow, *Zia* has arranged for us to visit more family for dinner. "No good you coming to Rome and being lonely."

As we enter the large family compound full of aunts, uncles, cousins, and boisterous children, it is confirmed that our romantic dinner in Rome will have to wait. At least, we are not lonely tonight.

The next day we meet our friends, the De Luca family. They tell us how quickly they made it from Abruzzo to Rome. I have driven this route several times, lawfully, and they have managed to shave off a third of the time.

Laughing, I tease Massimo, but he is eager to prove that he, too, is a law-abiding citizen: "When it said seventy, I never drove more than a hundred!" Yet he admits it is unsettling when he cannot discern which towns really have photo radar and which ones merely claim to.

Despite the fact that he rarely leaves the confines of his hometown, he will have to invest in a GPS navigator that warns of upcoming photo radar. Then he can arrive even faster! The only flaw with the GPS is that it doesn't tell you exactly how many feet prior to or after the speed camera you must remain law abiding.

We spend a couple of days with them and other friends who have arrived from Tuscany to join our "romantic" time in Rome. At the Pantheon, we are treated to choir music sung by a group of twenty German tourists. Next, I delight in champagne *gelato* at Giolitti's, one of Rome's most famous and oldest *gelaterias*. As always, it is packed, and our group adds to the chaos, as they study the multitude of flavors as if contemplating the solution for world peace. When they have made their decision, the counterman asks, "Would you like whipped cream on top?" inciting another long debate.

At long last, we all have our *gelato*, and we stroll by the brightly colored homes with ivy climbing up them, surrounded by moss-covered terra-cotta pots overflowing with flowers. We walk past the handsome trattorias with white umbrellas and tables outside. Tourists and Romans watch the good-looking world go by. Everywhere we turn, it is beautiful: stately buildings, grand piazzas, and quaint alleys. Even the faded, dilapidated buildings with crumbling stucco manage to look charming. We saunter through the enticing streets of Rome, arm in arm—Sofia and me, that is. She is clasping my arm tightly, pointing out what an enchanting city this truly is.

Romantic Rome

I pry myself away from Sofia to purchase postcards. An elderly man notices me sitting on the steps, writing. He approaches and asks where I live, where I am from, and, of course, whether I have any children. We chat a bit, and as I bid him farewell, he leans over and gives me two kisses.

"Uno per te" ("one for you") and *"portane uno in Canada da parte mia"* ("take one to Canada for me").

I smile graciously and bid him *arrivederci*. The minute he walks away, I check my purse to ensure that my wallet and camera are intact. All is in order, and I feel ashamed.

We stop at a local establishment for coffee and pastries. I go to great lengths in my Italian to order *caffè latte, molto caldo, mezzo caffè e mezzo latte* (*caffè latte*, very hot, with half coffee and half milk). *Well done*, I think, smiling at the man behind the cash register.

He looks at me, turns to the barista, and, without flinching, says, "One *caffè latte*."

I drink my lukewarm *latte* and console myself that according to Italians, this is the correct temperature it should be served at.

We head to the lively, colorful market, where they sell Murano glass necklaces. At the first stall, these cost twelve euros. We keep walking, and we find some for only three euros. I ask the vendor if they are original Murano glass.

He slyly smiles and says, "What do you think?"

Enamored by the price, I sort through them, nonetheless. For the same price, some come with boxes that say, "Genuine Murano glass, made in Venice." With great eagerness, we find our favorite pieces in boxes claiming to be real. At three euros each, for "real" Murano glass, we load up, and even friends previously not on the gift list will be given one.

Our final day in Rome is coming to an end. We brace ourselves, not wanting our trip to end on a sour note—for there is no doubt what Franco's next words will be. Sure enough, with a big smile, he suggests we all drive home in convoy. Everyone agrees with his fabulous idea, while David and I make excuses. They are confused, for just when it seems we are assimilating so well, we abruptly put an end to the day that could otherwise be "spent together," chasing one another on the highway. We bid them a safe drive home and make our exit, waving and blowing kisses as they stand bewildered.

We find a nice trattoria in the piazza, order two glasses of wine, and hold hands as we take in one last view of Rome's grandeur. Rome in the springtime, romantic at last!

Chapter 24

The Big Wig

Having realized there is no miracle cure that will take ten years off my face and ten pounds off my thighs, I do the next best thing—I go to the hairdresser with a picture of a woman who is ten years younger and ten pounds lighter than me.

The lumps in Grandma's and Grandpa's mattresses are slowly vanishing, as the economic crisis in Italy continues, but Giacomo's hair salon remains full, despite a color, cut, and style costing more than a day's wage. The concept of *la bella figura* is alive and well, and I want in on it.

I try to convince my mother, who is visiting and who is also a hairdresser, to accompany me to the salon in the center of the ancient town. In a moment of desperation, she has cut her own bangs with dull scissors, so that they now look like a set of teeth with half of them missing.

She refuses, insisting that hairdressers always cut her hair too short. I assure her that Giacomo is different. So we surf the Net for several hours and choose three pictures of medium-length hairstyles to bring him.

As we are about to leave, my mom chickens out and, almost crying, says, "No, they always cut my hair too short."

Finally, I persuade her.

Giacomo is wearing his compulsory tight black T-shirt that says, *Noi lavoriamo per voi* ("We work for you"). Yes, for me—and my hundred euros, that is. The salon's decor is modern, and we are seated in white leather chairs as we await our turn. Everyone knows everyone and happily chats away. Judging by their dress, this is the social event of the week, because they are all decked out in designer clothes, perfect makeup, polished nails, and even their hair already looks good. I feel out of place as the ever-practical North American, who also dressed for the occasion but in an old T-shirt and ratty jeans.

Giacomo sees me and stops cutting to come over to meet my mom, "the hairdresser," because I had told him about her.

"Your mother is beautiful," Giacomo says, "but with this current haircut she looks like Angela Merkel, the chancellor of Germany!"

My mom sits stunned, not quite sure whether this was meant to be a compliment or not.

He returns to styling a client's hair, as she bemoans the economic situation in Italy and her husband's loss of employment. He has been out of work for a while, with no hope of finding a job anytime soon. As she leaves, she says, "See you next week for my style." Cuts to their budget apparently do not include scaling back on hair styling each week or designer clothes.

It is my turn. I anxiously anticipate the end result, as I show Giacomo the picture I have carefully chosen. After my cut, I expect to be younger, thinner, bustier, and taller.

Giacomo studies the picture for a brief moment, then begins cutting. As he cuts, he chats uninterruptedly with friends and acquaintances strolling in off the street to kill time. Being Italian, he must maintain eye contact with them while speaking. He is also quite the ladies man and rushes over to greet each customer with a double kiss. I patiently wait for my transformation into a supermodel. He continues cutting and chatting, while I nervously survey the floor and the mound of hair collecting on it.

Giacomo finishes, puts some solution on his hands, and runs his fingers through my hair. Next, his assistant works furiously like a master with a round brush and curls and blow-dries my hair simultaneously.

My head is getting bigger by the minute. When she is done, she asks me to flip my head over and douses it in hairspray.

"Flip your head back," she commands, and I obediently do so.

"*Bellisima!*" Giacomo exclaims, as he rips off the cape and takes one last look at his creation, waving his hands at me as if I were the prize in a game show.

"Truly *bellisima!*" he says. Since he said that to the lady prior to me, who looked as if she needed a barber more than a hairdresser, I do not find comfort in his declarations of my beauty. He should learn to vary his expressions of appreciation for his own work.

I look in the mirror and feel as if I need a stiff drink before I am able to hand over a large sum of money.

"So, what do you think?" Giacomo asks.

Without that drink, I still manage to say, "I look like I have a wig on."

It appears big hair is back in style. I glance at the picture I brought with no bangs and very little layering and look at my hair—with bangs and lots of layers.

A silence engulfs the salon, as Giacomo and his assistant, Laura, and all of the customers stare at me.

"Don't worry, everyone loves Giacomo's haircut—two weeks later," Laura assures me.

Giacomo is evidently surprised not to receive the usual accolades. I gaze in the mirror and try not to cry, imagining the expression on David's face as this foreign woman enters our house.

I've always wanted to walk into a hair salon and say, "Do whatever you think." As I step down from Giacomo's chair several inches taller, I know the reason why I've never said that before. It would be the equivalent of telling my husband, "Follow that car."

The hairstyle I have and the one in the picture are worlds apart. Worse yet, I am still ten pounds overweight.

My mother is next, and although she has watched him cut hair and feels that he is a good hairdresser, she still approaches the chair like a lamb to the slaughter. She shows him the three carefully chosen pictures and explains that her head is like a *zucca* ("pumpkin") and launches into an elaborate speech in her practically nonexistent Italian, explaining what needs to be done.

She pulls a few strands up and down and out, and he runs his fingers through her hair, reassuring her that he understands.

She then commits her biggest mistake: she looks up at him and says, "I have the utmost confidence in you."

This is the moment that Giacomo mentally throws out the three pictures we carefully chose and feels as if he is given free rein. Thus, he begins to cut and cut and cut. He blow-dries the few strands left and says, "Voila!"

My mother feebly says, "Thank you, it is nice."

I am standing at the register, waiting to pay. Laura asks in a discouraging tone whether I would like a receipt, as if by accepting one I would be participating in a clandestine activity. My look of confusion provides the answer, and she quickly hands me one.

As we exit, my mother says, "What did I tell you? They all cut it too short! My nephew's newborn baby has more hair than me!"

"It will be easy to maintain," I say, trying to look on the bright side.

"Of course it will," she says, "when you have three hairs on your head!"

I drive home through the gorgeous Tuscan countryside and try to focus on the positive things in my life and not on my hair. "Hair grows, hair grows" will be my mantra for at least two weeks. My mom's as well.

Seeing the tears in my eyes, David tries to control his facial expressions but cannot. "Once you wet it, it won't be so puffy, right?" he consoles me, then looks at my mom.

Two weeks later, a miracle takes place—I am overjoyed! I love my haircut, and my mother loves hers. In fact, it is the best haircut I have ever had, and my mother feels the same. I am one step closer to the ever-elusive *la bella figura*.

Chapter 25

Doctor Dear

My poor mom came with a cold, and now David and I are left with a cold. We go to see our doctor, where we find out he has told patients his last joke. The "powers that be" prohibited him from practicing medicine any longer because he refused to use a computer. Now who would provide the masses with their daily dose of humor and the occasional prescription?

We pick a new doctor, based on free convenient parking. We go to his office and sit in the waiting room. He does not take appointments. Rather, one simply shows up. So, as each person enters the room, we greet him or her, make eye contact, and let the individual do a quick memorization of our faces. A vigilant mental record must be kept of those before and after us.

One lady makes the identification process easy: she has attempted to offset the ravages of time by wearing gold wedge shoes, baby-blue socks with white clouds on them, leopard print pants, and a brown turtleneck with a blue sweater over it. Flamboyant purple eyeglasses complete this memorable outfit. Her hair is flat ironed, and she's around seventy-five.

Miraculously, this system works, for the moment *il dottore* pokes his head out, the person next in order makes a beeline for the door.

Our reading of old magazines is regularly interrupted, as we greet those arriving and those leaving. *Buongiorno* and *arrivederci* are chanted umpteen times during the wait.

Our new doctor has an excellent reputation, and I can see why. My first visit consists of several background questions—him asking me, that is.

"Do you smoke?"

"No."

"Do you drink?"

"Not really."

"What?" he exclaimed, as if I had answered that I drink a bottle of a dodgy brand of whiskey every day.

"Well, you should!" he says. "Some wine with each meal is good for you."

With a response like that, how could he not be everyone's favorite doctor?

Going over my list of symptoms and considering his concluding diagnosis, I'm disappointed, because I'd spent hours online, self-diagnosing, and had come up with a host of pity-inducing illnesses, all of which have similar symptoms. General fatigue seemed to cover a multitude of them; oddly enough, none of the medical sites even hinted that perhaps I stay up too late watching TV.

David's cholesterol is slightly on the high side, so I inquire whether there is something he should avoid.

"Simple. Anything that is very good. Cheese, cold cuts, sausages, pretty much most people's favorite foods." Then, with an easy-going laugh, he elaborates, "I, too, have high cholesterol, but I take pills and eat what I want."

David flashes me a vindicated look.

Perhaps the doctor's lackadaisical approach will contribute to his long and happy life, despite his high cholesterol.

I leave with a prescription for rest, and David leaves happy as well, knowing that he has an ally.

Because all manufacturers have simultaneously made their print smaller, we next visit the state eye doctor. The waiting room is full of immigrants and elderly people. A very serious-looking man with thick glasses calls us in. He has me read a total of four different cards. I have not even proved I can read Italian when he says, "Okay, that is fine."

He moves on to David's exam and with record speed completes it.

"I could give you a prescription for distance," he says, "but it is so minimal, in the end it would be the equivalent of glass in a window." Oddly, he is bent on giving us the same prescription for reading glasses. "You could be a 2, but since your husband is a 1.5, let me make both of your prescriptions for 1.5."

I say that I would like bifocals, but he expresses disdain for them.

"Just drop your glasses onto the bottom of your nose when not in use, like I do," he says.

We leave with our "prescriptions," and at the pharmacy I pick up a pair of stock glasses—number 2. When I drop them to the bottom of my nose, I will officially be older than I ever imagined.

Chapter 26

Homeless Bound

Spring is in the air! Birds are singing, wildflowers and poppies are peeking up through the neon green of the new wheat growing. My hair is growing. Life is good.

Click!

David holds the receiver, too astonished to speak. Apparently, our landlord is not having a good day.

"I told him that our electrical outlet is broken, and he yelled at me and hung up!"

The phone rings.

"*Pronto*," answers David. "Okay. Thank you for apologizing. Yes, I will inform myself. But—"

No chance for rebuttals; however, an apology has been offered by our landlady.

"Well, then, I will have to inform myself," David says.

Though he gets dressed quickly, he picks out his outfit with the greatest of care, for he has noticed that the treatment he receives is largely based on his attire. He has vowed never to go to the *Comune* ("city hall")—or anywhere else—dressed in work clothes. Those clothes are reserved for places where only I can see him.

I survey my suddenly handsome husband and am grateful he is making the trip up to the *Comune*.

The BMW roars out of the driveway, and no doubt he will make it there in record time.

In record time, he has also returned and, in record time, is also back in his work clothes.

He must try to decipher Italian rental agreements. He places the comfy lawn chair directly in front of the wood stove, which is also smack dab in my way while I'm cooking in the kitchen. I use my better judgment and don't say anything. I let out a loud scream only when he inadvertently opens the wood stove door, and it touches the back of my knee.

"Aha! It is their responsibility!" David is pointing to the proof. Even with my limited Italian, he has proved it to me; now he must try to prove it to the landlords.

Armed, he dials. The *signora* answers. David is not looking for confrontation and keeps his tone pleasant. "Your husband told me to inform myself, and it is your responsibility—"

David has no chance to cite "by law section, and so on." The *signora* is not pleased. David keeps trying to get a word in edgewise but cannot. He puts down the receiver and in astonishment quotes the *signora*: "We really misjudged you. You are perfectionists! If you would like to leave, then the sooner the better."

It takes a moment for this to sink in. "So, we're being evicted?" I ask.

"They cannot legally kick us out, but she suggested they prefer we leave," David replies.

We look at the many improvements we have made to their house.

"Doesn't she realize how much we have done for them?" I ask.

"No," David says dejectedly.

Saddened by this turn of events, we try to figure out what to do next.

Not wishing to cause undue anxiety to the many visitors who are planning to come soon, we keep this secret and let them think we are sipping a glass of Chianti somewhere under the Tuscan sun. Because that is most likely what I will do today—make that two large glasses . . .

We search the local real estate magazines, and the first ad we find is not promising. "The villa is the perfect mix of the past and the present. On one side of the property you have the mythical past, whereas on the other you have the sound of the high-speed train that passes by."

I put down the magazine and find a website offering assistance. I sign up for information on homes available in our area.

The following morning, our previous agent, *Signor* Lippi, calls. It's a miracle, because when he was our agent, he never returned our calls. However, it has taken only twenty-four hours for him to find out we are looking for a new home and that we have not called him.

"I thought we were friends . . . ," he says, deeply hurt.

I muster up excuses, but within minutes I agree to his helping.

"I know of a couple of places, and *I will call you soon.*" Those were *Signor* Lippi's famous last words.

After much searching, we do the only sensible thing—beg, grovel, acquiesce, and by agreeing to confer most of their responsibilities onto us, we make up with our landlords. I try to empathize with them that at their age, it is not easy to manage so many properties, the husband has bad health, and so on. On the bright side, they never bother us, and I guess the new rule will be that we never bother them.

We renew our contract and paint the kitchen before our friends arrive, none the wiser. We plant a vegetable garden and fill all of the vases with colorful flowers. Our friends will find us just as they expected—drinking fine wine on the terrace, overlooking the charming hilltop town of Castiglion Fiorentino, in nothing short of paradise.

We are still awaiting *Signor* Lippi's call, several months later. We are deeply disappointed, because "we thought we were friends."

Chapter 27

Large Black Capital P

At my current age (thirty-nine, plus many, many months), I now feel that speeds above 30 miles per hour should be prohibited on all roads, including motorways. As per the video clip they showed us during driver's education, drivers must at all times keep both hands on the wheel in the 10/2 position. Changing CDs should be outlawed, and people found texting should be imprisoned for life. Before I venture onto any journey more than an hour away, I confirm that my will is up-to-date.

Despite this, David has phone calls to make, so I am the designated driver this evening.

I glance in my rear-view mirror. The impatient Italian behind me passes furiously on a solid white line, then brakes hard and almost comes to a complete stop as he turns right, into a driveway directly in front of me.

The speed camera is ahead, so I won't be the only one driving the legal speed soon, if but for a fleeting moment. I am not a bad driver—just a very lawful one. The only other people who maneuver similarly to me are student drivers, so indicated with a large black capital P on their back window (for *principiante*, meaning "beginner"), as are men and women over eighty driving twenty-year-old white Fiat Pandas.

Despite my terribly lawful driving, we arrive at the Neapolitan family's home. Their four-year-old son, Luigi, was rather concerned, because his mother had not had anyone over in two weeks. Finally, he asked her, "Is everything okay, since no one comes to visit us anymore?" Hence, our invite.

The table is laid with assorted Italian appetizers: prosciutto, ricotta, *caprese* salad with buffalo mozzarella fresh from Naples that morning, olives, and potato croquettes. The four-year-old's appetite is voracious, and I fear losing a finger if I get in between him and the prosciutto. Though only four, he looks seven; hence, I deduce this is not the first time he has eaten like this.

David is eyeing the last few potato croquettes and is about to take one when the kid pounces on them and grabs every last croquette. He shoves the next one into his mouth before he even finishes the first one. David and I exchange incredulous stares. Memories of kids having their *merenda* ("snacks") at Kids' Summer Camp come back to haunt us.

The parents laugh it off, but as the kid continues eating like there is no tomorrow, I ask, "Has he not eaten in a week?"

They all chuckle at my "joke."

Every so often, the parents forget themselves and speak in their Neapolitan dialect. I cannot comprehend a word, and neither can the kid, who has no idea what language they are speaking. He listens eagerly and tells his parents that he, too, wants to speak English like them.

Aware of what's coming, I think of a way out of tutoring their only child English. I remember Ed, in the book *Under the Tuscan Sun*, wanting to be reborn as an Italian baby—who wouldn't want to be?

As the mother continues to fuss over and stuff Luigi, I fast-forward forty years, as I think of the Norwegian commercial depicting an older Italian man, still living at home and being babied by his ever-doting mother. The commercial ends by encouraging those who don't want to end up like him to get a mortgage. Years ago, the legal age for a child to move out was sixteen. Yet based on my current findings, it appears that this age has been moved up to forty.

It's getting late, so I say, "We have a forty-five-minute drive. We'd better get going."

According to them, the drive home is much shorter, so there's no need to hurry off. A heated debate ensues over just how long it should take me to get home. I remind them that with the way *I* drive, *I* have a forty-five-minute drive home and must head out.

David directs me out of the narrow parking space, leans his seat all the way back, and says, "Wake me when we get home."

Hans, who also lives in our valley, leaves at the same time as us and follows us home. A half-hour later, our cell phone rings. David answers and looks behind.

There is Hans, phone in hand. "Tell your wife she is driving so slow that there is a backup of cars from here to Arezzo!"

I peek in the rearview mirror. There are no taillights ahead of me (drivers who had managed to pass me are long gone), but a very long line of shining white ones trails behind me.

I pull over, and within moments, Hans passes, tooting his horn several times and waving and laughing hysterically as he at long last overtakes us. The other cars follow suit. I conclude that I need to put a large black capital P on the back of my car; or else buy a twenty-year-old white Fiat Panda, as a courtesy to other drivers.

Chapter 28

Cinque Terre-rist

We had met Stefano through mutual friends while visiting Viareggio, with Barbara and Roberta. Stefano was tall, very tanned, handsome, and charismatic to boot. We got along famously, and more than once he invited the four of us to have exclusive use of his home and garden in the Cinque Terre.

It wouldn't be long before the girls yearned to see the Cinque Terre—or so they said. "Join us, you will have such a good rest. I guarantee it!" Roberta's words would be oft quoted during our trip.

The days were hot, and the sun shone faithfully. Having already hosted several guests, I felt that a small rest would indeed be in order. Besides, Roberta "guaranteed it."

We can't seem to avoid our usual hurried and stressed state when starting a vacation. There is much to do prior to leaving, and as always, we haven't given ourselves enough time. Roberta and Barbara will be waiting for us at nine—hence, our mad rush to meet them on time.

We finish packing, water our vast flower and vegetable gardens, feed the chickens, load the car, and by eight-thirty, I am sweating and frazzled. It will not be long before I have additional reasons to be stressed out.

Roberta offers to drive, followed by, "If we hurry, we can make it in good time."

It becomes apparent that rest stops and coffee breaks will not be on her list of priorities. I long for the days of leisurely breaks for greasy McDonald's breakfasts, accompanied by large American coffees—always a priority back home when taking any road trip.

Being Italian, she has to appease my hunger, but without losing time. Thus, she offers everyone food and takes some herself, acting like the perfect host, despite the minor inconvenience of needing to drive safely. She even keeps a vigilant eye on the guests in the backseat, to determine when to offer seconds.

Other drivers also seem convinced that God is looking out for them, as they make phone calls and text, while smoking.

Fortunately, Barbara has a small bladder. It will not be long into our trip before she insists we stop at the Autogrill along the highway. Barbara asks whether we will all go in or wait in the car.

"Are you kidding?" I ask. "Autogrills are the best part of a road trip. The Autogrill people should rule Italy. Of course, I'm going in!"

Seeing this may take longer than expected, Roberta reluctantly joins us.

Roberta and Barbara order espressos, while I foolishly order the cappuccino. I know they will down theirs like shooters, while standing, while I chug mine quickly, in order not to keep them waiting. Despite their protests, I insist on paying. As I search for my wallet, they again offer to pay. I keep insisting, all the while frantically searching. I take out the entire contents of my purse, but the wallet is not there. The girls pay the bill, while I panic.

We return to the car and take it apart. My wallet is nowhere to be found. We are an hour and a half from our home, and there is no turning back.

"What if we are in an accident? I have no documents; my health card is at home—"

David tries to lighten the situation, asking, "What are your last wishes? The three of us will remember to tell the doctor."

As he finishes his sentence, a huge truck crosses over into the merge lane, nearly side-swiping us. Barbara screams, and Roberta swerves out of its way just in time. Silence fills the car. There will be no more jokes about last wishes.

I left stressed. I travel stressed. Each time a truck manned by a wildly impatient driver flashes his lights, urging us to go faster, I recall that already broken promise "You will have such a good rest!" Hopefully, our host, Stefano, will take pity on me.

We arrive in La Spezia, on the Italian Riviera, home to Italy's largest naval base, and find Stefano waiting for us. He hops into his BMW convertible and says those dreaded words: "Follow me."

Roberta is intent on not losing Stefano, so she turns into one of the wildly impatient Italian drivers, honking at all interferences, while seemingly taking curves on two wheels. We drive up the steep, heavily forested hills to the east of La Spezia and soon arrive.

When Stefano told us that he had a house in the Cinque Terre, I foolishly assumed that (1) it was a house, and (2) it was in the Cinque Terre. Instead, we are introduced to Follo. The reason this name doesn't ring any bells is that only 0.0012 percent of Italians have heard of this place, and all of them live there.

The colorful homes wedged high up on the cliffs, with the smells and sounds of the sea below, are nowhere to be found. Instead, we are in Follo, whose Google search amounted to "Follo borders these municipalities . . ." I knew I was in trouble that very minute.

We are led to our accommodations, consisting of a main-floor bedroom, with another bedroom in the basement, rare in Italy, all shoehorned into a miniscule townhouse. We will certainly be "cozy" here.

Stefano immediately hurries us to eat, as it is time to go to the beach. With his dark tan, he looks as if he spends every free moment there. He has a very caring nature, and I hope one of the two girls will perhaps marry him, so that I haven't risked my life on the highway for nothing.

Stefano decides that David will drive his convertible, while he goes with the girls in their car. With my lunch still digesting, I get into the car and brace myself, as David, not knowing where he is going, must keep up with the car ahead. The curves soon get to me, as does the hot Ligurian sun beating down. I determine that convertibles are not my style.

Thankfully, we make a stop at one of the many focaccia stores. The aromas emanating from the shop are in themselves fine advertisement. I am amazed at the variety of focaccia: rosemary, onion, soft cheese, gorgonzola, and another dozen flavors tempt our taste buds. We each choose something delicious, and I reluctantly get back into the car.

Despite Stefano encouraging us to pass on blind curves, we arrive in Tellaro, a lovely, yet much less known, town on the Italian Riviera. I happily spend the day sunning and swimming in the warm blue sea, while David and Stefano catch octopus. Thanks in part to my new body (I blame it on my many guests) and the salty water, I float with ease. I lie on my back, looking at the ancient buildings in the distance. The earlier worries of the day are long since forgotten.

Dinnertime approaches, and Stefano proudly tours us around. The shore is lined with colorful seaside cafés, featuring outdoor tables with pretty flowers and white umbrellas. I suggest a drink and dinner while we enjoy the sunset, but Stefano has other plans. We must hurry home, because twelve people will be coming for dinner tonight. Italians obviously have a different interpretation of *exclusive use* of his home.

Roberta flashes me an apologetic look, no doubt recalling our conversation, when I said, "I'm tired of cooking. I want to eat out and relax."

Barbara had agreed, and, despite their tight budget, they had put aside funds for dinners out. Stefano also informs us that they are all learning English and would like us to teach them tonight. I conclude that nothing in life is ever really free.

Naturally, we help cook in the tiny kitchen and run the plates of octopus risotto down the stairs to the table in the basement. Afterward, Roberta, Barbara, and I carry the empty dishes upstairs and help Stefano wash them. Tomorrow will be different, I vow, as I dry the last platter.

We are jolted awake early in the morning by the lady upstairs, who has a penchant for wearing high heels on her ceramic floors, pacing and loudly conversing on the phone. I stumble out of bed, groggy, and find the girls in no better condition. Their sleeping quarters consist of a converted garage; hence, in the wee hours they could already hear the adjacent tenants talking, while revving their cars and working in their garages.

Regardless, this should prove to be a lovely day, because we will rent a boat and tour the Cinque Terre. I envision anchoring on our private beach, swimming in blue grottos, and leaving the hoards of tourists behind. Stefano gets off the phone and says we must hurry, because the others will be waiting. There will be eleven of us. Stefano was born to have an entourage. As per

Italian custom, rather than meeting directly at the port, we will meet at another location, wait the half hour to forty-five minutes for all to show up, and then madly follow one another, convoy-style.

Despite my vow never to be hijacked again, it is happening. David suffers the same fate and looks rather anxious sitting on the back of Stefano's scooter. We watch them weave in and out of traffic, with Stefano mostly looking behind to talk with David. Stefano's gentle nature has vanished once on the scooter. The chase continues through narrow alleys and winding roads, while David desperately clutches onto the back of the scooter for dear life. He looks as if he is going to throw up. Even though he is getting a taste of his own medicine, I feel sorry for him.

We miraculously arrive.

"So, how was the scooter ride?" I ask.

"Did you see the way he drove? He kept talking to me the whole time, making eye contact! I was scared to death!"

"You should have told him *occhio alla strada*" ("eyes on the road"). A line David knows only too well, for it is often quoted to him.

We wait for the boat in the seaside town of Portovenere. It sits on a rocky peninsula in the Gulf of Poets, an area once popular with writers such as Byron, Shelley, and D. H. Lawrence. Portovenere is on the Unesco World Heritage list for being an example of the ways in which man has been able to transform the environment, without altering the beauty of the landscape. Looking around with delight, I have to agree.

The picturesque harbor is dotted with brightly painted houses, and narrow medieval streets lead up the hill to a castle, while shops line the main street. The pretty cafés, with purple bougainvillea cascading down their walls, are filled with well-dressed Italians drinking *espressos* and chatting on cell phones, while tourists wearing T-shirts and comfortable sandals drink large beers.

A decrepit boat advertising tours pulls into the small harbor. I pity the poor souls taking that tour. Our boat will be considerably fancier, because I was told it has a bar and a bathroom.

Stefano warmly greets the scruffy-looking man jumping off the boat. "Ciao!"

My heart sinks. Leaving behind the elegant boutiques and the chic bars of Portovenere, the eleven of us cram into this boat. Visions of me sipping a martini disappear, and I pray I won't have to use the bathroom. As the boat chugs out, diesel fumes fill the air and our lungs. We arrive at our first destination, Byron's Cave (where the poet Byron used to swim). We could have reached it on foot and still had clean lungs. A dozen students study poetry on the rocks.

The men and I jump out of the rocking boat into the blue water of the sea. The men swim to the nearby caves, but I stay a safe distance away, worrying, keeping vigil, as the rough waves smash against the rocks. The other women remain in the boat: between diesel fumes and the rocking, the women are fading fast. Despite fearing the men may drown, I'm enchanted by views of the ancient ruins of Doria castle. Built in 1161, this imposing edifice showcased a lavish life of privilege.

We jump back into the boat, making it sway some more for the benefit of the women, who are about to vomit. We journey toward the Cinque Terre, five splendid fishing villages surrounded by agricultural terrain. The pastel-colored houses perch on rocks and cliffs, as a testament to the ingenuity of people who have overcome the disadvantages of steep, uneven terrain. Conversely, the cultivation of vines on terraced cliffs is a testament to their love of wine.

The Lonely Planet says about the Cinque Terre: "Set amid some of the most dramatic coastal scenery on the planet, these five ingeniously constructed fishing villages *can bolster the most jaded of spirits.*" I'm not sure whether it's the scenery or the prospect of exploring the town's narrow alleys with their shops and boutiques, but somehow the women are revived.

We spend the day jutting in and out of the Cinque Terre's small harbors and entering quaint shops, while stinking of eau de diesel. We stroll past the many souvenir stands awaiting their next prey. A rather enterprising soul has purchased dozens of coffee cups and with blue magic marker has scrawled Cinque Terre across them. I imagine the look on the recipient's face on receiving one as a gift from an unsuspecting—and possibly blind—tourist.

Manarola

We arrive back at Portovenere, exhausted and ready to return to Stefano's "house in the Cinque Terre." David insists that someone else accompany Stefano home on his scooter.

Yet the party is not over. Stefano has invited everyone for dinner. He says his "Bimby will make us all a fabulous meal for next to nothing, so why spend money in a restaurant?"

Bimby sounds like a cheap prostitute to me, but it is known in the United States as a Thermomix. Or, as the *Wall Street Journal* introduced it, "Meet Bimby, the Robot Chef."

I discover that while Bimby cooks, she does not wash or scrub the vegetables, nor does she do dishes. Perhaps my version of a Bimby would have been more helpful.

Because the others are "guests," Stefano cooks, while Roberta, Barbara, and I do double duty as waitresses and dishwashers. And so ends my weekend of "rest at Stefano's house in the Cinque Terre."

Chapter 29

Chick Magnet

David climbs the steps of our house, and, in between huffs and puffs, he laughs as he shows me the magazine cover from the local supermarket. I gasp. A sixty-year-old farmer with a strong resemblance to David, wearing a white straw hat far too small for his head, proudly holds a hoe in his hand and stands in the middle of a field of cabbage. I also notice (but do not mention) that this farmer's arm muscles are much larger than David's.

"Yup, this is what I will look like in twenty years!" David says, with a grin.

I suddenly realize that my vision of my husband, in a crisp white shirt with black slim-fit pants, may just be that: a vision.

Meanwhile, David seems quite content with his destiny as he looks at the cover (perhaps he, too, has noticed the farmer's bulging muscles). To confirm my suspicions, the latest issue of *Practical Poultry*, a gift subscription from friends, has also arrived in today's mail.

I will most likely keep wearing *Zia*'s primary-colored wool socks in the winter; hence, we will be a perfect match for each other. Being happily married does not depend on what one wears, even when in Italy.

I brace myself for seven hours of cleaning Eric's rental home, Tillia, to prepare it for new guests arriving later this afternoon. While the money is nice, I resent having to give up the pool for the week to paying guests.

David tends his garden, and although the tomatoes he planted from seeds have not taken, in a strange twist of fate, our lavender bush is sprouting tomato plants from the compost we deposited there. David promises to remove them, but I am dubious.

I return home from Eric's to see that I'm not the only one who has been busy. David has purchased three new hens to eventually replace Roberta and Barbara, because they are slowing in their egg production. He has also put his fine cabinetmaking skills to use in building a hen-size ladder leading up to an eight-foot-high window out of the pigsty where the hens are kept and another ladder leading down to the fenced-in grassy area. He found some old roof beams, leaned them on either side of the window, and nailed twelve-inch pieces of twigs across to give the hens something to grip as they make the arduous climb.

I watch, convulsed with laughter, as he tries to train the hens to go up and down. They stare at the custom-built ladder leading to freedom but display as much enthusiasm as someone needing two knee replacements being forced to climb Mount Everest.

Roberta and Barbara are dissatisfied with their new roommates and are clucking in protest. During an urgent phone call, David's mom advises leaving them all inside together for a while to get accustomed to one another. David locks the little door, and Roberta lets us know that she doesn't like her new associates or staying indoors. She stands at the front of the gate, as if clucking, "Get those birds the hell out of here!" All of the hens join in the protest, while I go for a walk to escape the noise.

Luciano from the village greets me and informs me that he is in the know about our new hens. Stefano, his son, is with him but is rather depressed. He finished beautifully restoring a house next door to his parents' home, but his girlfriend of seven years has decided she needs to see the world first, whereas he wants to stay put. Stefano reasons that many foreigners have lived elsewhere and toured the world, yet end up in Tuscany. So why waste time traveling, when this is the best place on earth? When I look around, I see that he does have a point.

Armies of sunflowers in the valley have turned their faces toward the sun, while olive groves glisten on both hillsides. I walk along the fitness trail and arrive at a bench where the kind city of Castiglion Fiorentino has provided instructions for the stupid among us. The first instruction is *If you are tired, sit down*. I am not tired, but I sit down nonetheless. After taking in the views and contemplating life (i.e., wondering whether the chickens have calmed down), I return home to find David in the field, surrounded by all five chickens.

As we head out for dinner at our friends' house, he gathers the furiously clucking hens into the pen.

Dinner conversation revolves entirely around the chickens. Recipes are shared, and David is encouraged to purchase a sickle to cut fresh herbs for the hens—in particular, stinging nettle. The rest of the process involves chopping and boiling. Everyone chimes in with more home remedies requiring the purchase of specialty food items. They deem the stairs too strenuous, and plans are made for new accommodations.

There is a sane one among the lot, for Marcello pipes up and sarcastically says, "And on chilly evenings, go in with a blow-dryer to heat up their little butts."

I believe that for a brief moment, this seems like a viable option to the rest of this group.

Finally, David says, "I'm not cooking them three square meals a day, especially meals that require hours of manual labor reaping crops." Then, his final declaration: "You know, you *can* buy eggs at the supermarket!"

And thus, our scintillating dinner conversation is brought to an abrupt end.

Back home, our hens have called a truce; the three new hens are crammed together, sleeping in the box that is for laying eggs, and Roberta and Barbara are queens of the castle, huddled together on the perch.

Chapter 30

Bello Marcello and "the Albanian"

David had done odd jobs for our previous landlords, who came from Naples—they laughed hysterically when David offered them a customer satisfaction guarantee.

"But we are in Italy!" they said. Being from Naples also explained why they insisted he stay for lunch and dinner each time he did work for them.

He also tried a bit of restoration work, but after receiving instructions about how to find electrical wires from his uncle, who was a restorer—pretty much by trial and error, or literally hit or miss 220 volts—David chose life, forgoing future renovation jobs. David was simply out of his element working here.

Yet Marcello is desperate; he needs the work, and the job must be finished quickly, so, for friendship's sake, David offers to help him out.

Marcello is a true artisan, and he is not one to hold back the truth. His honesty is manifest even on his website, as he quotes John Ruskin: "All quality work must have a price. . . . Beautiful things are not obtained by means of compromise . . . and cannot be produced with a small cost." While this site may scare off any potential North American customer, Marcello is confident that lovers of art are inclined to pay. And indeed, he has found a willing customer in Siena.

He picks up David at 7 a.m., because they have a one-and-a-half-hour drive. The automatic coffee machine grinds, and the smell of espresso fills the kitchen. I hear Marcello, wide awake and his usual amiable self: "Thirty percent of Italians voted for a comedian! What would you say if thirty percent of Americans voted for Woody Allen?"

I laugh when I hear David remind him that we're Canadian.

Marcello is well dressed and shaved, and I catch whiffs of strong cologne. Meanwhile, David just hopped out of bed with his eyes barely open and grabbed work clothes that had been shoved in a drawer. Marcello loves working in Siena, because they always pay him, unlike several other jobs he has done.

The Sienese are motivated by a strong sense of keeping up appearances, so all he would have to do is spread the word that so-and-so did not compensate him, and he would quickly receive his wages. Marcello wishes all of his jobs were in Siena. "Living in Italy is so hard these days that when people ask what I do for work, my answer is 'I live in Italy.'"

David, eager to help Marcello with his financial situation, suggests, "What about a work exchange program? Maybe with your skills, you could switch with someone in another country, like the teacher exchange program?"

Marcello gestures animatedly with both hands. "Most of the time I have no salary. Find me someone willing to work for nothing, and it's a done deal." He then breaks into laughter.

Marcello is fifty-five and is often several months behind in rent payments and has to approach his mother for an advance. His lighthearted spirit and cheerfulness never diminish, despite his trials, and he is truly to be imitated.

"The Africans standing outside the supermarkets selling things or begging make more than I do some days. Maybe I'll join them," he says and doubles over laughing again.

Marcello is not alone. We have a number of friends who have not been paid in months and eventually give up waiting and quit. The notices posted on a bus shelter confirm the depth of the crisis: people with degrees are searching for work as tutors, nannies, cleaners, and so on.

They down their espressos, and David grabs the lunch and snacks I prepared for him. He kisses me and heads out.

I release the hens into the field, because they are still not used to the steep ladder, and I collect any eggs we have been gifted. Despite the early hour and sleeping neighbors, Marcello honks as he leaves our property.

They arrive in Siena, and Marcello puts on his work clothes. He shows David the technique he has mastered, and they start the job. Marcello is applying a cool gray resin floor in a sizable apartment in the historical center. Although the building is centuries old, the new owners want a contemporary look, mixed with the ancient stone on the walls. The views from the terrace overlook weathered rooftops, while the flooring inside will be contemporary. The little girl's room will have fuchsia-colored resin floors. Though the work is difficult and messy, Marcello is continually cheerful.

"Time for a coffee break," Marcello says. David gets his lunchbox and starts to pull out snacks, while Marcello leaves the room. David is already eating when Marcello returns, cleaned up and elegantly dressed. He looks somewhat disapprovingly at David but says nothing.

"Let's go!"

David follows, as Marcello leads him down narrow alleys, past neighbors conferring emphatically, to a modern bar in the heart of Siena. They order espressos and down them in seconds, yell, *"Arrivederci!"* to the barista, and head back to resume their work.

Siena

This scene is repeated several times during the day, with David waiting for Marcello to dress and undress for their lunch at a hip restaurant and then for their afternoon espresso break at another chic bar.

On the one-and-a-half-hour drive back, David eats the snacks and lunch I have packed.

David returns home, and, on catching sight of him, all of the hens run to him. I give him the egg count for the day, and he says, "Good girls!"

The job in Siena is not finished, so David will assist Marcello the next day as well.

That evening Marcello calls with a message for David: "I'll be there at seven. Only tomorrow, please don't dress like an Albanian!"

David could have sworn Marcello appeared embarrassed to be seen with him!

The following morning Marcello arrives, bearing gifts of assorted chocolates. Apparently, his wife, Elda, had overheard him and thought he might have offended David.

David laughs and gratefully accepts the chocolates. He kisses me and leaves the house, unshaven and in his best work clothes, albeit quite wrinkled. He's hoping Marcello will make another derogatory comment, resulting in more gifts.

Chapter 31

Speeding with Seniors

Because I am up, I take advantage of the cool morning for a one-hour walk into town. En route, I pass a large stone house standing majestically in the sun. The blue gray shutters hang crooked, and the steps leading into the house are overgrown with moss and ivy, confirming its abandonment. Views of the hilltop town of Castiglion Fiorentino grace the home on one side, while the castle of Montecchio looms grandly in the distance. My imagination leaps into the undeniable dark history of the previous inhabitants, and I think up elaborate theories about how the house fell into such disrepair. Sadness overcomes me, as I contemplate the likelihood that someone's dreams did not come to fruition. Throughout the Tuscan countryside, you will stumble across many such homes and, no doubt, many such dreams abandoned.

Castle of Montecchio

As I continue, the views are arresting, and my mood soars. The world seems perfect, as I walk through the scenic countryside with ancient stone homes covered in roses. Windowsills filled with red geraniums or petunias brighten most balconies.

A man pruning his garden warmly smiles and greets me. A young boy around seven plays outside, alone. Holding two sticks, he seems content with these simple "toys." It's a scene from a world long gone. The boy smiles at me.

Touched, I compliment him. "What a nice smile you have."

"Arrghhhhh!" yells the formerly sweet child, as he lunges at me with the sticks, attempting to poke my eyes out. He is feisty and keeps at me, all the while maintaining a smile. The shouting incites the German shepherd next door into a frenzy of ferocious barking, and suddenly the world no longer seems perfect. Or perhaps the dog will attack the child, and all will be well again. Just kidding.

I arrive at a tiny ancient church. Outside, a handwritten note is posted on the door: "The Lord calls anywhere . . . but surely he won't call you on your cell. So please turn it off before entering the church."

In town, colorful shutters take turns opening in the narrow alleys, as the inhabitants slowly awaken.

Historic center in Castiglion Fiorentino

The only places "teeming with life" are the bars, full of elderly men who each buy one coffee and then spend hours socializing.

Castiglion Fiorentino's historic center, still surrounded by medieval walls, has some of the loveliest views to be found. Regrettably, though, the main piazza is a parking lot, mostly servicing those who visit the post office. I stop for a coffee in a bar under the nine-arch loggia overlooking the valley. I sit outside and leisurely enjoy a cappuccino and the views and avoid contemplating my one-hour walk home. Inside, the bar is packed with people hovering over the main counter. Perhaps Italians take their coffee standing up because it's much easier to keep gesturing, gesticulating, and talking that way.

I'm ready to embark on my hike home when I see Lorenzo, or, rather, he spots me. Even though we have known him for a couple of years and run into him several times a week, he has forgotten my name.

"Ivanka," I remind him. He then accusingly asks me if I remember his name, as if I possibly had the nerve to forget it. Five minutes later, he refers to me by another name. Lorenzo is close to eighty and under five feet tall; hence, I must look down to speak with him. He has thick white hair, rosy cheeks, and a slight waddle when he walks. After some pleasantries, without thinking, I mention that I'm going to walk home. He insists on driving me.

We attempt to reach his car but are hampered by the fact that Lorenzo is a professional monologuer. We walk a few feet, then he stops. "Do you know what took place in this town right here?"

He then launches into an elaborate speech, arms flailing, as he jumps back and forth, excitedly recanting every bit of historical minutia. And he cannot remember my name! He could be a stage actor, single-handedly playing all of the parts. I would rein him in and walk several more feet. Then the opera act would begin all over again.

Lorenzo cannot multitask, because he must stop frequently to expand on his already expansive story. He asks me another question, which I answer in two sentences or less.

He says, "I will give you my version of the answer," which is the one-thousand-sentence version, complete with Dolby stereo. At the conclusion of his long monologue, he lets me know that "people love conversing with me."

If both of my legs were broken, and I had to crawl the entire way, I could have dragged myself home by now. Peacefully, at that.

We finally approach the parking lot, where a poor unsuspecting soul stops to ask for directions. Lorenzo launches into a set of complex instructions that, if obeyed, would land the person in northern Germany, rather than the restaurant he is looking for nearby. The man smiles, and Lorenzo takes this as an opportunity to educate him on the beauty of Tuscany, while slipping in several times that he has lived in Switzerland and that, unlike the villagers here, he is a man of the world.

Lorenzo pauses, and I mentally urge the man to flee.

He is on the verge of saying, "Thank—" when Lorenzo pulls out a map, around five feet by two feet (about the same size as Lorenzo) and, in the most convoluted way, explains the directions. The man leans forward and listens, displaying the patience of Job. If I were to discover that this man is a serial killer, I would let him off for good behavior and time served. Finally, Lorenzo is satisfied that the man can get to his destination and releases him.

I get into his deeply cherished old six-cylinder BMW sports car.

"I want to show you what this car can do," he says.

"I will be sick if you drive too fast," I warn him. I don't mention it's my nerves and let him assume he may be cleaning up after me. He assures me I am in good hands.

Comedians always joke about old people driving slowly, yet my destiny is only to drive with maniacal seniors. Though I have noticed a curious phenomena: there *are* slow old people on the roads but only when *I am behind* the wheel. Then they all make an appearance, mindlessly cutting me off, drifting in and out of traffic, oblivious to the fact that they cost the general public thousands in brake pads each year.

Lorenzo tears through the streets, inches from stone walls and people's front doors, and gets me home in record time, leaving me unsure which would have been the lesser of two evils: being in the car listening to his interminable speeches for any longer than necessary or risking my life in a high-speed race.

When David and Marcello return, I tell them, "Inspired by my walk, my next book will be about the lost souls of abandoned homes."

"Great idea!" says Marcello. "It would entail lots of research and interviews, but it could be quite interesting."

David, not believing that this would make a fascinating read, says, "They moved. THE END."

Perhaps I am destined to write about maniacal seniors. In which case, Lorenzo came in handy today.

Chapter 32

To Be or Not to Be . . .

It has been a lazy summer. While here, Eric met an Albanian family. He left us a note asking whether I would be willing to give them my cleaning job, because they are in desperate need of work. He repeated several times that they have five children. He left the decision up to me, but how could I not give them my job? I didn't want to have five hungry mouths on my conscience. Eric is a good man, and he gave us work when he saw that we needed money. Time to pay it forward.

So, life has slowed down considerably. We no longer have Eric's guests dropping in for visits, drinking several cappuccinos, and staying for hours—because, after all, they are on vacation. We will save a small fortune in coffee beans. Thankfully, David will still look after the pool, so, when there are no guests, we can use it.

The forty tomato plants are heavy with bright red tomatoes. David has built a wooden box with a terra-cotta bottom and a screen cover to dry batches of tomatoes in the hot sun, ready for jarring in olive oil. This wooden contraption makes us the envy of our neighbors.

The huge garden demands a good chunk of David's day but brings him great pleasure, watching the fruits of his labor grow, then sharing them with our friends who live in town. The hens follow his every move.

Each morning I collect the eggs, usually three but on rare occasions four, happy to be able to make a frittata with produce from the garden and fresh eggs.

To avoid the heat, I go for my walk up the hill early each morning, stopping to write when so inspired. Dario and Peppe, brothers, who are too old and ill to walk up (Dario claims to have only half of a heart), chug up the hill in their tractor to their small plot of land, where they have a vegetable garden and an olive grove. Each morning they offer me a ride. I smile and say, "No, thanks," and Dario kisses my hand and takes this opportunity to use the few English words he knows.

Dario sees me scribbling and asks, "Are you writing?"

"Yes," I reply. "And when I become famous, then so will Pergognano."

They look at me, confused. Perhaps they feel it already is famous.

On returning home, I write on the terrace in the sun, and my skin becomes a deeper tan color. Soon I'll blend in with my Italian friends. I'm just missing the flowing white linen skirt and the pouty mouth, for my dream to be realized.

So, David works in his garden, with the never-ending weeding, while I research and write stories for my second book. At mid-morning, I put my work aside to start cooking, because I invited some friends over for lunch today: Marcello and his wife, Elda, and a friend of theirs, Julia. Now that the first book has been published, they have all been warned that I might write about them.

Our Tuscan hilltop town in the distance makes the perfect backdrop for the elegant table setting, with a burnt umber tablecloth skimming the ground and several flower arrangements, artistically composed of pink roses with olive branches, cypress branches, and ivy cascading down the vase.

I cook a simple meal, yet it appears lavish, and I manage to finish preparing it before the guests arrive. I even washed my hair, and I have on makeup and clean, elegant clothing.

With the weather perfect, we sit happy and satisfied after lunch and, in this ideal setting, listen to Marcello discuss Italy's demise. A quasi Martha Stewart moment, at long last.

David, as if in a period film, takes Marcello on a tour of the grounds and shows him our prized chickens, which David has trained to jump for food.

We women stay behind and chat, while browsing through home décor magazines. Julia, whom David and I had met on a few occasions, looks around reflectively and says, "I have a few regrets in life."

Not knowing Julia very well, I assume her regrets are not dissimilar to those of others of her standing—people who have left behind their families and their home countries in search of a better life in Italy. I innocently ask, "What would those be?"

"I have always wanted to be a sniper. I regret never becoming one," she says nonchalantly, as if regretting being a sniper was the same as regretting not being a doctor or a humanitarian aid worker.

I suppress the reassuring speech I had mentally composed, about it never being too late to follow one's dream. Naturally, not knowing how to console someone for missing her calling as a sniper, I stare with my mouth open. All I can muster up is, "Oh!"

She doesn't flinch and elaborates on why she would have made a good sniper. Her sense of loss is so deep, you'd think she had lost a child, rather than an opportunity to deprive someone else of one. As if to prove her fine marksmanship to us, she closes one eye, stares intently into the field, and makes a shooting noise, while using her hand as if it were a gun.

In the middle of her reflections, David and Marcello appear with a dead chicken on a shovel.

Julia is taken aback and pauses in her sniper story.

Though absolutely distraught by the sight of Barbara, lifeless on a shovel, I am also relieved not to hear any more of Julia's regrets.

"I saw her two hours ago, and although she seemed a bit sluggish, I can't believe she died," David says sadly.

He and Marcello go to bury Barbara, and Julia takes this opportunity to continue her saga.

That evening we break the tragic news to my in-laws about Barbara. Julia is not the only one with regrets. My in-laws regret that because Barbara died of natural causes, there will be no broth from her.

Chapter 33

Lamb-asted

David's prolific tomato crop this year means it's time to make sauce. This is now a family affair, so we embark on the three-hour trek to my in-laws' house in Abruzzo.

"Since she's not laying eggs anymore, don't forget to bring Roberta," my mother-in-law tells David. She fears Roberta, too, possibly dying of natural causes; thus, the family would miss out for a second time on some broth.

My heart breaks. Knowing Roberta's days are numbered, I sneak her—an *Italian* hen, after all—her favorite food: Parmigiano Reggiano cheese. I cut it into small slivers and watch her eat heartily. This will be a secret.

In the car, I squawk more than Roberta, who sits quietly in her box. David's speeding apparently doesn't bother her. She knows this route. It was only two years ago that she traveled *to* Tuscany with us from my in-laws'.

As is our custom, we stop in Norcia to pick up wild boar and liver sausages. The shopkeeper owes me three cents change, so instead throws in another sausage.

We pass through towns with curious names, Quintodecimo ("five-tenths") and Favalanciata ("launched fava bean"), and arrive in my in-laws' tiny village.

Giorgio is in the dining room with two old men, one slightly more ancient than the other, whom we discover is the son. All three are red faced, having downed half of a large plastic coke bottle filled with boiled wine. An assortment of stale cookies sits on the table. Maria thinks they are a sufficient complement to the boiled wine concoction.

After the men leave, the remaining biscuits get wrapped in cloth napkins and the more privileged pieces into clean paper napkins. Maria looks at me innocently, as though she has not been wrapping and re-wrapping these biscuits for months. For the remainder of our visit, this odd assortment of stale and surprisingly non-stale food items is presented as an after-dinner selection to accompany the nightly grappa.

Roberta has been placed in the hen house and is getting along fine with the others. I cannot even begin to think of what awaits her. A friend had warned me never to name our chickens.

***

We are woken abruptly the next morning. Maria is up and in the kitchen, donning her ancient pink highly flammable polyester housecoat. Many threads have unraveled, and I fear she will trip over them.

She wanted us to get up early, because she has to pick up her passport at the Questura, which deals with matters of immigration.

If the overcrowded parking lot is any indication of how many are waiting ahead of us, then we're in trouble. Many people wish to remain in "the Promised Land."

As we approach the hoards of people standing around in no particular order, I wince, recognizing this will not be quick. Every nationality is represented: Chinese, Africans, Albanians, Romanians. There are no numbers, no queue barriers, just mass confusion. We find our place in what we believe is a line and vow not to budge, despite the bodies pushing, shoving, and slamming against us.

I reminisce about Canada and those plush red velvet cords ensuring law and order that I had taken for granted all of these years. People walk in and march ahead of us. The personnel behind the glass are getting frustrated, as are those on the other side. Soon the staff begins yelling for order.

I leave David and his mom to battle with the masses, while I wait in the hallway outside. Along the corridor, a series of pictures hangs with a notice stating, "Pictures not valid." The Italians have forty examples of unacceptable photos. These include a Bedouin shepherd, a man with a cowboy hat, a Shiite

Muslim woman with only her eyes showing, a man with a toque askew on his head, a woman with extremely large dark sunglasses, and a man posing sideways. The Bedouin shepherd makes a second appearance with a fully covered face, along with a woman whose hair covers her face and a man wearing a straw hat. Nor is it acceptable to submit a photo of someone else for your document. I amuse myself, as David and Maria finally approach the counter.

The agent gives my mother-in-law her passport and notices her birthdate. "You really look good for your age," he says.

She laughs. "I lived in Canada for many years. The cold there has preserved me."

The supermarket will be our next stop. Maria surveys the beef and dismisses any from an animal born in France, even though the cow later moved to Italy and was raised and butchered in Italy, according to the label.

My mother-in-law is intent on serving lamb for lunch and asks the butcher to bring her some. Yet each piece he presents does not meet with her approval. He keeps returning, and the whole lamb is slowly being reassembled, piece by piece. I can now picture it grazing on the grassy hillsides. As more limbs of the lamb turn up, Maria completes the picture in her mind and informs the butcher, "This small lamb looks like it was tortured in a chamber for the entirety of its brief life; deprived of a mother, food, and water."

She then asks for Roberto, the head butcher, as if he can miraculously produce a worthy lamb. In the end, three butchers become involved in her quest. The lamb is now almost completely reassembled, while Maria suspiciously eyes the scrawny leg.

Maria is without shame, as she loudly concludes it did not get enough vitamins. She leaves the giant pile of meat and the three butchers with blank stares. I, too, gaze in astonishment.

The butchers suggest a rabbit, but she dismisses that, with more theories as to its upbringing, much to the bewilderment of the multitude of people in line behind her.

Miraculously, Roberto suggests she return tomorrow, because they are getting a new shipment. I cannot imagine that they would want her back.

David can no longer endure the combined smells of *baccalà* (dried cod), meat, and strong cheeses and informs us he is going to the cleaning aisle to breathe the toxic fumes there instead.

On the drive home, we are treated to a dissertation on how to identify good lamb meat. Maria admits to using restraint, because she wanted to say the lamb looked as if it had been aborted. A lecture ensues on this lamb's life and how it was taken away from its mother too early.

We have six more errands to run, which will invariably take far longer than they should, as Maria fails to inform David of the turn and then loudly declares, "We should have turned back there!"

With the lamb deemed unfit and Maria's racist views toward the cattle, we have buffalo mozzarella and prosciutto from Parma for lunch, followed by her homemade gnocchi in fresh tomato sauce and items from the fridge that passed the sniff test.

Pleasantries over lunch include vivid details on how to slaughter a chicken.

I finish loading the dishwasher and am ordered to take a nap.

On awakening, I say one last goodbye to Roberta. While they "do the deed," I will get my hair colored at the hairdresser's. She has a small shop in the back of her parents' house. Inside, a plaque placed above patches of dark, thick mold says, *Santa Maria del Carmine Guarda nostra familigia* ("Saint Maria del Carmine, watch over our family"). If they are still alive with all of that mold present, then a miracle indeed has taken place.

Several women sit around chatting. They agree that Ida's husband is a true gem, and while one daughter takes after the impossible mother, the other is truly the father's child. Speaking on behalf of the entire nation, none of the women care that Berlusconi runs around with underage girls; they only mind that he picks them as cabinet ministers. His personal affairs are between him and his wife.

I return to my in-laws with a new cut and color and with several small-town secrets, as well as solutions for all of Italy's woes.

Several days pass, and with Maria's state-of-the-art processing and canning equipment, we make hundreds of bottles of tomato sauce to last another year; hence, it is time to go. My mother-in-law is busy packing our car with a virtual grocery store. Roberta, gruesomely dismembered and frozen, is back in the car, returning to Tuscany—surely having traveled more than most Italians. It will be a sad batch of chicken soup. Rule number one: *never* name a hen.

Chapter 34

Table Nazi

The resilience of elderly Italian men and women never ceases to amaze me. We stop to pick up our weekly supply of sparkling water in Monte San Savino. An older lady, seeming fragile, sits outside on a hard chair, reading a Ken Follet novel. While David returns last week's empty bottles, she lugs out the crate of full bottles, refusing to let David help her. Her movement is slow and deliberate, like Tim Conway's elderly character on the *Carol Burnett Show*. Each week, the price changes. When we finally had the nerve to ask why, she frankly replied, "Don't trust me. I never remember the price."

We head to Warren and Delores's place. They're an American couple living in a lovely villa in the countryside just outside the ancient town. Because Delores is visiting family in America, rather than enjoy her wonderful cooking we will meet Warren in a restaurant in Sinalunga.

David needs to make a phone call, so I drive. We approach the restaurant, and Warren takes the first available parking spot. I want to stop behind him, but David, always convinced a closer spot awaits, urges me to drive on. This time he is correct, and we see a large parking place.

"Wow, this is great!" I say, as I smack the curb with the aluminum rims of our BMW. David cringes. He steps out to survey the damage, while I finish parking.

Meanwhile, Warren is engaged in a heated discussion with an Italian couple that has exited a white Panda.

"You did this!" a lady yells, after eyeing Warren's Mercedes.

Warren calmly inspects her car, then his. "I'm sorry. I did lightly tap you, but there is no way I did that." He points to the scratch and the deep dent that have been there for some time.

His thick American accent clinches her dream of having her bumper fixed. She continues to rant, as her husband looks at his feet.

Warren stares blankly, unsure what to do. The *signora*'s hopes are quickly dashed when David, with his Italian face, appears.

David takes one look at the bumper and concludes, "This happened a long time ago."

The woman, taken aback, recants, "I *was* tapped. I just want an apology for being tapped."

Warren apologizes again, and she hurries off in a huff.

We enter the restaurant with a sense of gloom. The two of us have the only wide-open parking spaces in all of Italy, and we both manage to have separate mishaps within feet of each other.

The restaurant, Il Forcillo, is empty, aside from one couple and their child. They have a "seat yourself" policy, so we do. I pick a table in the corner, and we begin to relax, laughing about the events of the day.

"If you hadn't come along," Warren says, "I'm sure she would have forced me to take out my checkbook."

"Yes, you'll have to work on getting rid of your American accent," says David.

The waitress arrives from the kitchen and "greets" us. "You have taken a table for five. There are only three of you!"

She physically helps us up by grabbing my coat and Warren's arm and waltzes us across the room to a table set for three. Warren bursts into a fit of laughter at being moved in an empty restaurant.

"This is perfect, isn't it?" the waitress asks.

The one place I hate to sit in a restaurant is near the bathroom. Yet I must have a sign on my head that reads, "Looking for a small, cramped table, near the bathroom, please. The closer the better," for that is inevitably where we end up.

I glance around the vacant restaurant and then at her, as she waits for my response.

"Actually, no," I dare to answer this threatening-looking lady of about seventy-five. I risk something happening to my meal, as I explain my disdain for a table in close proximity to the bathrooms.

"Well, then, I have another solution." She marches us back to the table where we started and moves the adjoining table over a foot, leaving us now sitting at a table for three. The couple we had been sitting next to, then had *not* been sitting next to, and are now sitting next to again, no doubt label us "crazy *Americani*."

Back where we started, we await our menus for quite a while and fear we are being punished. At last, the elderly *signora* emerges with three plates of bruschetta drizzled with olive oil and places them on our table. The table is cramped, but we dare not touch anything or move it to the empty table beside us.

Two men enter and survey the room. They have no aversion to being next to the toilets, as they seat themselves at the table for three we recently vacated. The waitress emerges from the door leading to the kitchen and scolds them for sitting at a table for three. Without a word, they obediently follow her to a table for two.

"They need a sign that says 'Seat Yourself until We Reseat You,'" says David. This sends us into an uncontrollable fit of laughter. The neighboring couple surely concludes we are mad.

The menus arrive, and we order. The waitress seems to have forgiven us and even smiles. Hence, I ask whether it would be okay to change the order in which my food arrives. Seeing the look on her face, I say, "Never mind, bring the pasta first and then the meat second."

She looks at me as if a grave sin had almost been committed. She waves the menu dramatically, saying, "Thank heavens! If I did not do it in the correct order, the kitchen would have killed me!" She runs her finger across her throat several times, accompanied by sound effects.

I smile weirdly, figuring that is my best bet.

The restaurant slowly fills. Thankfully, most groups of two appear to know the rules of seating, and no emergency interventions are required.

The tables are almost all occupied, except the table next to us. The ancient waitress cannot keep up, so a smiling man emerges from the kitchen to assist.

"Is everything okay here?" asks the incredibly handsome waiter, whose name I imagine to be Fabio.

"Yes, everything is very good," I say. My pasta, *pici with cacio e pepe,* a thick spaghetti-like pasta smothered in pecorino cheese and pepper, is the best I've ever had.

He notices we are cramped with all of the dishes we ordered, so he moves the other table back next to ours, clears some space, and places some of our plates on the once again adjoining table.

I sit uneasily, fearing the waitress's reappearance—she may be small, but she's feisty.

I want to warn him by duplicating the gestures and sounds of the *signora* describing what the kitchen would do to her, but there is no time.

She comes over. "Is everything okay here?"

"Wonderful," I say guiltily, as if we had moved the table ourselves.

Her eyes shift from us to the adjoining table. I want to yell, "Fabio moved it!" but wisely refrain. She walks away, looking back suspiciously at us.

We speed up the pace of eating and keep an eye on the door, praying no new customers come in, lest we get Fabio in trouble with the kitchen staff.

A customer would like to greet the chef, so Fabio says, "Tell mamma to come out. Someone wants to say hello." Out emerges a sweet, smiling eighty-year-old wearing a white apron—supposedly, the killer in the kitchen.

We forgo dessert and coffee, taking our leave while the going is good.

The meal was wonderful, and, thanks to the feisty *signora*, we can also boast that we got "a room with many views."

Chapter 35

We "Chianti" Find a House!

Our rental contract is up for renewal. Though we love the stone farmhouse and its vast grounds and have made many dear friends, we decide to try a new adventure and move closer to Florence. We inform our landlady, with whom we currently get along great (because we never ask them to fix anything). Although she is disappointed, the house may come in handy for her son, who is living in London but will be getting married soon.

We recently returned from Canada, having spent several months working like dogs and learning the hard way that the Chinese may not be the best option for quartz counters and that not everyone claiming to be a home stager has good taste or access to furniture from this century. Perhaps our brains are fried, or we are true gluttons for punishment, because we start looking for a new place during the height of summer vacation in August, when the entire country virtually shuts down.

The few agents who answer their phones are upset that we dare call during this time, saying, "I don't mean to be rude, but I'm on vacation . . ."

We patiently wait for real estate agents to return to work, so we can find a place to live by the fifteenth of September—the date we told our landlords we would move out.

We line up a few places and will meet *Signor* Rossi in the small town of San Pancrazio in the hilly wine region of the Chianti. The first stop is a sprawling villa from the sixteenth century, and it appears the owner is also from that era. The elderly lady, with a demeanor denoting noble descent, quickly informs us, "The prime minister stayed in this villa several hundred years ago."

After viewing the apartment, we conclude the prime minister's sojourn there was the apartment's best, and only, selling feature. Mere vestiges of a glamorous bygone era remained, because the furniture had seen better days, and "recent" renovations imposed on the kitchen in the seventies were out of place.

Noticing our lack of enthusiasm for the first apartment, the noble *signora* takes on the role of real estate agent and hurries us to another wing of the enormous villa, much to the chagrin of *Signor* Rossi. She unlocks the door and lets us in. "The kitchen, as you can see, is fully equipped."

Though massive, it resembles a kitchen where a dozen servants cooked meals for their lord before modern conveniences were invented. Dishes sit unwashed in the stone sink and on the counter, along with the remains of food, as if someone left in a hurry.

We are next led down a long corridor to a great sitting room with domed palatial ceilings and several seating areas, making it worthy of a setting in a period film. Visions come to mind of butlers serving tea to distinguished guests enjoying a piano recital. The rooms are endless, and so is the tour, with accompanying history lessons. We are painstakingly shown each room, oddly with clothes strewn about on unmade beds.

"The place is currently rented weekly," says the *signora*, "but we would prefer to lease it long term."

The unsuspecting tourists must have left for the day and have no idea we are prancing amid their dirty laundry and unwashed dishes as they tour the Chianti.

"These are the gardens," says the *signora* and swings the door open for us to admire the grounds. A large Italian garden with roses and boxwood hedges appears. It, too, has seen better days, as has a swimming pool with murky water in the distance. It is like an Italian version of *Sunset Boulevard*. I expect Max to open the next door. There is something so sad about the place, bygone days of a bygone era.

David and I made a pact that we would not waste our time or the time of the owners if we have no interest in renting a place. However, that is easier said than done. As the *signora* sings the praises of the house, we look for a way out. It is warm outside, yet the apartment feels cold and damp.

"We fear heating it may be very expensive." As we speak, we inch our way out, also fearing the tourists may return at any moment.

The *signora* has no such fear, for she launches into a lengthy sales pitch on how heating with GPL (propane) is not that expensive. Having lived in an old house with GPL heating, we know better and depart. The *signora* follows with the real estate agent. His long face reveals that he knows we're not taking the place. In fact, it has been for rent for more than two years, and his lack of enthusiasm while showing us the property was justified.

We meet our next agent, a young man, Oscar in San Casciano, and he drives us in his Austin mini to the next house. He zips around corners and over hills, seemingly catching air over speed bumps. He suddenly brakes for radar traps and, once past them, reverts to breezing along at a good clip.

He takes us to see several homes in the area, none of which are suitable. He has a few more, but since the sacred lunch hour is approaching, we will part ways and meet up after we eat. David and I ask for a recommendation and go to a quaint trattoria in the town of San Casciano.

The next house, in Mercatale, is enormous and six hundred years old. It is divided into four apartments, two of which belong to our prospective landlady and the other two to her brother. She lives a half-hour away in Florence and stays in her portion of the house only on weekends and during the summer. The apartment for rent is where their father used to live and is considerably cheaper than other places the same size. Our portion does not have any workable land, but a large stone courtyard and loggia would be for our use. I picture us sitting under the arches, drinking wine and watching the sun set. An ancient stone wall built on an incline protects us from the small street in front of the house. The views are stunning, with rolling hillsides covered in vineyards.

The apartment is fifteen hundred square feet, boasting beam and terracotta brick ceilings slanting to fifteen feet on one side. The rooms are sizable and well laid out. Two open fireplaces adorn the living room and the dining room. A dark, medieval table and hutch, seemingly taken from a castle, overpower the dining room. Meanwhile, in the bedroom we find beds that the seven dwarves must have slept in, with low metal frames in bright red. Someone has an unusual concept of "mix and match."

Oscar points out the laundry area, but it's soon evident that his clothes get washed by way of a miracle, because he knows nothing about washing machines. He shrugs and confesses, "My miracle is my mother." He owns a flat in town but rents it out and lives with his parents.

Despite the furnishings, I am sure this will be our new home—until we enter the kitchen. Someone with a real love of dizzying colorful tiles decorated the room, because tiles line every wall of the kitchen and cover the counter. And that counter was designed for someone seven feet tall. Yet although the counter is ridiculously high, the fridge is only about a foot tall, and there is no oven. My heart sinks, while Goliath would rejoice.

The place was advertised as furnished, thus should include a full kitchen. (In Italy, a place classified "unfurnished" does not include a kitchen but, rather, only pipes jutting out of the walls. Even when one sells a home, the kitchen does not usually remain with the house, to which our friends Anna and Francesco will attest, having moved and retrofitted their own kitchens four times.)

Because I love cooking and spend hours in the kitchen, we return home no further along in our search than the previous week.

Our friends are more optimistic than we are. Marcello has found the solution: "wear high heels in the kitchen," while Chantal is more practical and emails me, suggesting I "get used to cooking in platform shoes."

Chapter 36

Arrivederci

After more searching on the painfully slow Internet and making dozens of calls to agents, we have lined up more potential homes, this time in the countryside closer to Florence. The agent is in her late fifties and is decked out in a low-cut black clingy dress. She, like many other Italian women, has discovered the maximum support, minimum coverage bra. Expensive jewelry adorns every part of her body, making me wonder if Tiffany's has been robbed lately. Accompanying her is an assistant whose sole purpose appears to be opening doors for us, when the agent waves her hands and orders her to do so.

The first house is steeply priced at twelve hundred euros and is a shrine to the seventies.

The next house appears more promising, with gorgeous views, but the small second bedroom is overshadowed by a bizarre wooden boxlike structure. The agent, as if selling me on a "unique feature" of this home, explains that it is covering a stairway but says that we could add a mattress on top and get a stepladder, so that it can be used as a bed. I envision my elderly parents and in-laws risking their lives to get into bed at night.

A *fienile* ("hay loft") also has lovely views, but, the owner divulges, "It is very private here. I saw the previous tenants come out here to sunbathe in their bathing suits every day." Hence, we realize it's not private enough.

We hurry back to the Chianti area to meet Oscar before the lunchtime cutoff. Because time is running out, we take another look at the apartment with Goliath's kitchen and decide it's the best of the lot. Since we don't have jobs with contracts here, we will have to provide the landlords with another type of guarantee that we can pay our rent. We give them proof of Canadian income, and in the end they accept it, figuring that even an Italian with work today may not have it tomorrow, so they are safer going with the *Americani*.

Delores and Warren have decided that after living for thirty-five years in Italy, they will move back to the United States. We purchase several items from them at rock-bottom prices, ever grateful, because I can ask for the medieval table and buffet to be removed, as well as the dwarves' beds.

David's sister Filomena and her Canadian husband, Joe, moved to Italy last year and have come to help out, due to the prodding of my mother-in-law, who insisted Filomena bring our three hens to her place, because we cannot take them with us. Thus, Filomena and Joe will spend a hundred euros in gas to drive three hours to our place and then to the in-laws to deliver the hens. Incidentally, one hen costs about seven euros.

Though we are moving only an hour and a half from our previous town, the going-away parties begin. Our neighbors Enzo and Giovanna have us over for one last unforgettable Tuscan meal.

Many good friends help us load up the rental truck, and, much to our astonishment, the twenty-six-foot truck is soon chock full. Rocco, our original landlord, from Naples, will drive the truck for us, while David and I, with a car also full to the brim, will try to keep up.

I leave with tears. We had so many fond memories here. Even the bad ones have become good—trying to find work; then, sadly, finding work; and dealing with mischievous mechanics, cunning real estate agents, and various mishaps. Now these quirky experiences merely seem humorous. I take one last look at the stone farmhouse and the prolific lavender we planted and am grateful for the time we spent here. I hope our new place will be equally paradisiacal, though I'd better invest in comfortable high heels to cook in.

***

We manage to keep up with Rocco, thanks to imposed speed limits for trucks, and arrive at the house. Our landlady awaits, gives us the keys, and provides a quick explanation, along with "hinting" at how often the floors should be cleaned: "So when you wash the floors each week . . ."

Rocco kindly stays to help us unload the truck, and eventually the large house is filled with furniture and boxes. Though we work tirelessly all day, we barely make a dent and call it a night.

***

The shutters are closed, and the room is pitch black. It appears to be the middle of the night, but what is all of the honking about? Barely awake, I open the shutters. A maniac speeds past the house, beeping frantically. It's only 7 a.m., so I go back to sleep. Minutes later, another lunatic honks, as if part of a wedding procession. By 8 a.m., we have figured out why this house was priced considerably lower than others. The small street is also a main street that narrows to one lane on a curve directly in front of our house. Drivers have one of two options: to warn oncoming traffic by honking a good distance away or to slow down. Everyone prefers option one.

My nemesis: the narrow road on a curve

I had asked Oscar whether this was a high-traffic street, and I now realize that either he is not familiar with the area or lying must not bother his conscience.

For the next hour, the honking is relentless, and as the bus passes by, I longingly think back to my peaceful existence back in Toronto, a city of six million. Because we have spent countless hours searching for a house, we know this is the best place for now. We hope today has more traffic than normal; hence, we unpack and set up the house. On a brighter note, I get my exercise for the day, as I raise my arms to chop vegetables at the towering counter.

Our landlords come and move the unwanted furniture from our apartment into a cantina below us, the size of a large apartment, which is packed solid with furniture.

After several days, the honking does not diminish, and I have to laugh, as "hilarious" friends back home sign their emails to us with "Beep, beep! Honk, honk!" When you live in the Chianti, no one has any sympathy for you. Chantal suggests looking at the views in between honks.

We make the best of it and decide to go to IKEA to shop for kitchen appliances and cupboards—at least, we can do something about that. My mother-in-law refuses to let us spend money on someone else's house and within a couple of days has arranged for her nephew to drive her old kitchen cupboards and appliances up to us. She joins him in the van, along with Filomena, and they drive four hours to bring us everything from her kitchen, including the oven and the fridge and enough food to fill it—even eggs from our hens.

They stay for lunch, which she has brought most of; then they take a nap and cram into the van to head back to Abruzzo—yet not before letting our neighbor know he should do something about all of the honking.

The apartment itself is really beautiful, and we start to make it home. Our phone and Internet are installed, rather quickly. However, the phone company has assigned us a number that belonged to several businesses that no longer exist. Yet their websites still post our number. So, in addition to the mad honking, our phone rings incessantly, only it's never for us. The views, the central heating, the beautiful apartment . . . I chant this regularly, trying to look at all of the good.

We settle in, and as October approaches the rains begin, and we discover the roof leaks in nine places. Buckets, bowls, and rags are scattered about our apartment. Guests currently visiting sleep to the sound of gentle rain falling—into a bucket next to their bed. Our landlords are apologetic, but the roofers cannot begin work until the rains stop. A week later, it clears up. The terracotta roof is large and old and will need extensive repairs. The crew of workers is eager to finish, hence arrives early to begin the banging above my head that will go on for two weeks. The landlord is also having major construction done to his yard, so the roar of loud machinery nicely harmonizes, while the chimney sweep joins the chorus with his loud vacuum.

I think of what my mother always says, "This, too, shall pass," and laugh, knowing she is right.

Chapter 37

A Day in Florence

I accept that I do not, nor will I ever have, an IQ sufficient to decipher the Italian bus system. I console myself, knowing that neither does the driver nor the man at the bus information center. So instead, judging by when the house rattles the most, we conclude what time the bus outside our door leaves for Florence.

Early one morning, we depart for a leisurely day of sightseeing in Florence. The large bus edges past only inches from the homes on one side. On the main road, an eighteen-wheeler transport truck traveling in the opposite direction flags the bus driver to stop and asks for directions. They chat for a long while. Surely, had they been discussing the meaning of life, the conversation would have ended by now. The two women behind the bus driver each offer an alternate route, inciting lively debate from other passengers, along with their concern on how to turn the large truck around. The bus driver is also worried; thus ensues a second debate on how best to do this, with the two women offering the most solutions.

The man in front of us, evidently on a schedule, even if the bus driver is not, finally yells, "Hey, get a move on!" With a deep sigh and a shrug, the bus driver shifts into gear, and we are off.

We stop in San Casciano, and a number of Africans board the bus. They are from one of the many newly opened refugee homes, formerly hotels, and are housed there while they await their immigration hearings, hoping for residency documents. Ironically, this area is nicknamed San Cash by many a rich expat.

Squeezed in the heavy traffic, the bus makes its way through a mad roundabout as we enter Florence. Miraculously, the bus arrives on time; perhaps breaks for conversation are incorporated into the schedule.

We pass a wall where someone scribbled graffiti: "Why is it called tourist season if we can't shoot them?"

Aside from that, the city appears welcoming, lit up and sparkling for the winter festival of lights. An opera singer performs in the Piazza della Repubblica, while expensive bars along the piazza attract dark, handsome men in slim-fitting suits and over-the-top dressed women toting large dark sunglasses, plenty of fur, and enough perfume to induce a coma in anyone with chemical allergies. The presence of older ladies with long jet-black hair and plenty of cleavage confirms we are in Italy.

We window-shop and spend hours lingering in the bookstore. We walk the cobblestone streets and discover a small restaurant serving delectable sandwiches for lunch. I order the Brie, *pancetta*, and arugula *schiacciata*. Personal space is nonexistent, and I feel very cozy snuggled up to the guy next to me.

A tourist asks to use the bathroom. The owner, wearing a mischievous grin, opens a trap door in the floor, lowers a set of stairs, and motions for the woman to enter. The rather large woman apparently does not suffer from claustrophobia, as she climbs down the narrow stairs. The entire restaurant is the size of some North American bathrooms, so I cannot imagine how tiny the underground bathroom must be.

Afterward, we mosey through the International Food Fair in Piazza Santa Croce and purchase, of all things, cheddar cheese.

After a wonderful day, we catch the bus home, ultimately grateful to have this convenience. We arrive at the station, only to discover a bus strike in progress—affecting our route, among others. Overhearing our panic, an older gentleman, who lives in a nearby town, finds an alternate route for us and himself and calls his wife to pick us up from there. Another man joins us, and the four of us happily chat on the ride home. This kind man works for a bank in Rome from Monday to Friday, then joins his family in the Chianti countryside on weekends; he says it keeps his marriage fresh. He has five more years until retirement.

The bus drops us off in an empty field in the middle of nowhere in pitch darkness. Soon a car approaches—thankfully, driven by his wife. Though David and I brace ourselves for the long hike home, they insist on driving us right to our door. We are truly touched by their kindness, and by the end we are like old friends, laughing and enjoying one another's company. We tell them to drop in anytime.

Meanwhile, today's events have confirmed my suspicions—I never will be able to decipher the Italian bus system. Accepting that and learning to go with the flow get us one step closer to being Italian.

Chapter 38

See You Later, Navigator

I've made friends with a group of Italian women who have learned English. They are very outgoing and vibrant, like many Italians. Three of them hail from other parts of Italy, while Monica's family is Tuscan and has moved a total distance of three miles during the course of five hundred years.

We meet at the main square in a nearby town; then we will travel together to join up with another friend. She had eventually relinquished her address when I insisted we could easily find her with a GPS. Only now do I realize that all of the GPS in the world could not help our group get to our destination, even though it's not far away.

Four middle-aged women squeeze into the car, along with Andrea, an adorable eight-year-old boy with dark hair, large brown eyes, and a face that lights up when he's spoken to. I wonder what this child could have done to deserve an afternoon with us. Thankfully, he *is* with us, being the only capable navigator in the car. The rest of us could not point north if our lives depended on it.

Confusion prevails, as all of us women simultaneously instruct the driver with different directions. To add to the chaos, Rita is loudly chatting on the phone, while intermittently shouting directions. Monica, in the backseat, suggests her own version of the right route to take. It's like attending an A.D.D. convention, with everyone on speed.

Worse, our driver thinks driving is a team sport and relies on her passengers to notify her when it's safe to make a turn, to reverse, and to merge. Thus, several frantic women supervise each movement of the car by yelling, "Go! Stop! Not yet! Wait!"

Andrea, nicknamed the "pocket navigator," also obliges the driver. Thankfully, this little eight-year-old is not strapped into a seatbelt and is standing next to his mother in the backseat when he suddenly shouts, "Stop before you hit the vase!"

Arianna slams on the brakes, giving Andrea a good jolt, but, thankfully, we avoid colliding with the vase. I add large non-moving objects to my list of things to fear when it comes to driving with Arianna.

Rita, now off the phone, engages Andrea in a game that includes hand gestures, loud noises, and joyful shouting. I worry that with the little kid so distracted, we may hit another big object.

As if there is not enough noise in the car, the rain heavily beats down on the metal roof. The windows fog, and finally the driver has an excuse for driving as if blind. I close my eyes.

Soon the heavy rain makes driving impossible, so we pull off to the side of the road. Andrea, meanwhile, stops playing and carefully studies the map to figure out a route for us. The rain eventually stops, and after we all agree it's safe for the driver to pull out, she follows Andrea's latest directions, and we arrive at our destination.

Our friend greets us, saying, "And I thought you would never find my house!"

The women all pipe up, insisting it wasn't that hard. I look at Andrea and wink. He knowingly winks back. Thank heavens for pocket navigators!

Chapter 39

The Color Gods Must Be Crazy

We'll soon go back to Canada for a visit, so, to comply with unwritten Italian beauty laws, I will go to a salon, to keep up *la bella figura*.

Yet as always, mischievous *bella* Italia has something else in store for me.

Giacomo is too far away to create a hairstyle I have *not* requested from him; thus, I will try, hopefully not by trial and error, to find a hairdresser nearby.

The economic crisis apparently has not reached this salon, because it is packed. I'm told they can take me if I'm willing to wait. Because we leave in two days, I wait.

I am not really sure where the kid came from—perhaps he was watching cartoons somewhere—but he commands, "Follow me." He leads me to a back room, seemingly for untouchables, with one lone chair and a mirror in front of it. As the kid struggles to put on black gloves, it dawns on me that this tall, lanky, post-pubescent boy is going to do my hair. He continues his fight with the gloves, and as the gloves are about to win, he gives one last shove, the plastic gives, and in go his bulky hands. He moves behind me and asks, "Ready?"

Ready for what? I wonder but meekly say, "Yes."

I show him the hair color I would like, and he calls one of the hairdressers. She glances at the picture I have carefully chosen and confirms that I would like medium blonde.

"Yes, just like the picture, medium blond," I repeat for emphasis.

"No problem." She returns with a paste, plops it on his tray, and exits, leaving me and the kid on our own.

I make conversation, but soon realize the kid has trouble multitasking so it's safer if I refrain. His clumsiness makes me suspect this is why they have banished him to this room. As if to confirm my suspicions, he drops another object and almost knocks over the tray with the hair dye. He has smudged the dark hair dye on my face and suddenly looks horrified to realize he hasn't applied cream to my face, facilitating the later removal of this dye.

He never does anything quickly, so he saunters over to get the cream and, at the same snail's pace, applies it. My confidence plummets, as he keeps yelling to someone in the other room for instructions. After an eternity, all of the hair dye has been applied. He clumsily combs it through, pulling out gobs of hair. I wince in pain. Finally, he is done and takes his leave.

The loud swearing of rap music and multicolored strobe lights "soothe me," as I wait and wait and wait. I cough loudly, hoping someone will remember me. A bell rings—the color gods in the other room hear it and call out, "Lorenzo! Lorenzo!" but he is nowhere to be found. As I begin to picture myself hairless, Lorenzo shows up. Maintaining the same level of ineptitude, he washes my hair.

"Would you like it cut?" he asks. As he drops the comb, I forfeit a much-needed cut and skip straight to the styling. How wrong can he go with that? I soon discover how wrong.

Every Italian hairdresser I've been to is very adept at using a round brush with a blow dryer to turn my North American hair into a mound of sexy, bouncy curls—Lorenzo now being the exception. He turns the brush one way, tangles it, and then cannot get it out of my hair. He tries to discreetly pull it out, but when that fails, he uses brute force. Trying not to scream in agony, I hope they won't charge me when I exit bald.

Miraculously, Lorenzo finishes, and, miraculously, he has managed to style the remaining hair into a mound of sexy, bouncy curls, albeit my hair is a light burgundy color.

As I pay, the cashier asks for my details, because she would like to register them for next time. I muster up the courage to tell her it is not the color I had asked for: medium blond. This is almost burgundy.

"I'm sorry, but I don't think you see well," responds the hairdresser who mixed the color. "It's the lighting in here."

As the days pass, I discover it is "the lighting everywhere." Regardless, everyone, including my family and my Canadian friends, loves my new hair color. Maybe that mischievous *bella* Italia knows what she is doing, after all.

Chapter 40

Cultivating Saintly Qualities

The benefit of living on a street with trucks passing by becomes obvious when there is an earthquake. While others scurry in a state of panic, we simply assume another large truck has driven past and nearly missed the house. Thus, we calmly go about our day, oblivious to impending doom. After we assume several more trucks almost miss the house, we realize we are feeling earthquake tremors. News reports alert us that we are we are very close to the epicenter in Campoli. Though the house rumbles and shakes slightly for days, our landlords reassure us that after six hundred years, the house is still standing, so not to worry. Nevertheless, we contact friends in the area, who suggest having our bags packed, just in case.

Thankfully, all shaking has stopped, because our friends Colin and Esther will soon arrive from Canada. Since ignorance is bliss, we won't even mention it.

We had warned them about the noise, and, to be polite, the first few days they downplay it. In fact, they are glad that the road less traveled is actually not that—and that the succession of cars starts honking at daybreak, forcing an early start on touring, so Colin can get more photographs.

The traffic subsides at lunchtime—the sacred hour for Italians and for me, too, as I revel in the peace that will be interrupted only after digestion takes place.

I prepare lasagna for lunch. The Rana noodles called *sfogliavelo* are divine—naturally because, as Rana advertises, it uses only fresh *Italian* eggs. I heed the directions. Cooking time is fifteen to twenty minutes; then the package states this will give me just enough time to set the table. I let David know that I will set the table today, because I have been specifically instructed to by my lasagna package.

I place a blue-and-white checked cloth on the table next to the stone shed with red roses growing up against it. Being first and foremost a photographer, Colin is so enchanted by the views that he pays no heed to the occasional truck zipping by. He sips his wine and gets up every few minutes to hopefully get "the shot."

After several weeks, I'd given up on walking here. I was afraid to risk my life with each step on these narrow roads. Yet David, motivated by a never-before-seen little belly, discovered a new route that involved few life-threatening stretches. Now, along with our guests, we stroll behind our house and through the rolling vineyards, with their green leaves awakening in the spring. We arrive at the Castello di Gabbiano, where Colin is rewarded with wisteria in full bloom, climbing up the turret of the castle. After touring the castle, the rest of us are impatient to move on, but Colin, taking dozens of photos, has lost himself in "the zone."

Our restlessness, and hence our lesson in cultivating patience, continues during the entire trip, because there are simply too many beautiful spots in and around the area where we live, and Colin is compelled to capture them all. This endless photo shoot can make even a sane person wish she lived in an ugly suburb.

The Chianti Region

That evening, I roast a chicken with fresh herbs from our garden and serve it with potatoes and wild fennel, harvested and dried from our fields in Castiglion Fiorentino, with freshly shelled seasonal peas as a side dish. I serve *gelato* from the supermarket after dinner. Esther is impressed that even simple foods have so much more flavor here.

On Monday, we take our guests to the San Casciano market. Esther eyes several scarves, while the vendor, hoping to clinch a sale, says, "This color looks great with a tan."

I laugh and, in Italian, let him know that "Thanks to her British background, Esther is as white as a ghost and will remain so all summer."

He begs me not to translate that to her, but I do anyway. Esther has a good laugh and, regardless, purchases the scarf.

Colin, intent on taking more pictures, has Esther and myself pose beside a pair of hanging underwear, the largest pair of underwear known to mankind. *Maybe that quintessential image will be "the shot,"* I think.

"The shot"

That evening we take them to Badia a Passignano, a little gem of an area, and eat at L'Antica Scuderia. Esther has the truffle and *burrata* (fresh Italian cheese made from mozzarella and cream) pizza, while Colin chooses the leek, sausage, and *burrata*. An excellent choice, because, according to the *Huffington Post*, "You need more *burrata* in your life!"

Chapter 41

The Amalfi Coast

Colin and Esther have booked a place for us on the Amalfi Coast. I take enough pills to knock out an elephant, put on my blindfold, and lean back in the car, ready to start "my vacation."

As David drives along the highway, Esther reads her e-book, while Colin sadly watches many photo opportunities pass by.

Orvieto is one of those places that we heard we should visit and planned to visit but never did, for the same reason that it took us six years to stop in Norcia—namely, always having to arrive at my in-laws' place by the sacred lunch hour.

"Hello, Orvieto. Goodbye, Orvieto," we would chant, as we zipped past it, ensuring we'd reach *Zio's* house in Rome by noon. This time, with no older men awaiting our arrival (and, more important, the arrival of their lunch), we finally stop, eight years later, at Orvieto.

The town sits in an exalted position, high on volcanic rock above the valley floor, and overlooks the Umbrian plains dotted with olive and cypress trees and vineyards. Orvieto's well-preserved old town center does not disappoint, neither us nor Colin. It has a dreamy feel to it, but that could also be attributed to my drugs.

***

We travel through the narrow, curvy roads of the Amalfi Coast and arrive in Conca dei Marni. Our hosts await, warmly greeting us. The husband insists on helping me with my suitcases, and as he lugs them down a hundred stairs,

I am grateful I let him. After brief instructions, they insist we call them anytime we have an issue; then they disappear.

We must be the first visitors of the season, because the house smells damp, having been closed all winter. The furnishings are basic, and the owners' obsession with artificial flowers is confirmed throughout each room. Puzzles and pink and green doilies in frames adorn the walls.

The master bedroom has a balcony furnished with a white plastic table, chairs, and two loungers. Yet the stunning views make up for all of the school projects decorating the walls—as long as we look out the windows, we can give this place a five-star rating. The coastline is endless, with sheer cliffs and homes that seemingly dangle from them. It amazes me to see the tenacity of those determined to live by the sea in this inhospitable setting. The bright-colored homes stand in stark contrast to the blue sea. As evening approaches, lights shimmer from the homes on the mountainside.

When the sun rises, I hear the familiar sounds of home: loud honking, but exponentially more of it and for a prolonged period. I look out the window and see a large bus trying to round a narrow curve of the mountain, with a car unable to move out of its way. The frantic driver of the car angles the car forward, backward, and almost sideways but is unable to get clear, almost hitting the stone wall barrier. In the end, the bus driver runs out of patience, signals for the driver to get out, and maneuvers the car out of the way. It dawns on me that the numerous blind curves on the Amalfi Coast foreordain that honking will be part of my destiny.

We check out the area and walk up the steep stone stairway that leads to the main road. With each step I take, everyone notices an ever-present squeaking.

"It's your shoes!" says Esther.

I walk another few steps and realize it *is* my shoes. I laugh. I will be haunted by noise wherever I go. As if on cue, a bus drives by and honks.

The sun gets hotter, and the pleasant morning walk to the sound of squeaking shoes becomes grueling. From afar, the homes jutting on cliffs appear glamorous, with their spectacular views of the sea, but as we get closer we see that not everyone has profited from making money on the world-famous coast.

The Amalfi Coast

We arrive in Ravello. Not to be missed, although we missed them, are the Gardens of Villa Cimbrone. While Colin spent hours taking photos at the gardens of Villa Rufolo, the rest of us spent the morning cultivating qualities of endurance, forbearance, and patience. However, now the waitress at the pizzeria insists that the gardens of Villa Cimbrone are the ones not to be missed, so, already having perfected the above qualities, the rest of us decide to split up and meet Colin later.

For dinner, we check out two restaurants from *Trip Advisor*. The first one, in a valley, is dark, empty, and ominous. The hairs stand up on the back of my neck, and I worry that some sort of dangerous business is being conducted here.

"What if I'm taken into white slavery?" I jokingly say to the others.

Esther assures me, "You are far too old for that."

Villa Cimbrone

The second restaurant, Le Bontà del Capo, is closer to home. We take seats on the terrace, and a waiter, Antonio, with long dark-blond hair and blue eyes, appears. Colin and Esther feel miffed because he texts while they give him their orders. They are convinced there will be no food arriving, and if it miraculously does, it will not be what they ordered. Ironically, Colin and Esther are device addicts themselves.

Esther asks whether they serve a red beer. The waiter, who manages to possess the almost impossible combination of charm and a vacant sort of indifference, replies, "My wife is blonde. So we serve only blonde beer here." And he continues to text.

The food arrives soon thereafter: the *arancini di riso,* fresh grilled sea bass, a mixture of fried seafood and vegetables. Everything is delicious and reasonably priced.

"I'm shocked! I was sure he wasn't paying attention to what we ordered," says Colin.

"You dumb-dumb!" is David's eloquent response. "He was inputting your order into that phone-like contraption."

We tell the waiter the story, and he says, "The last time that happened, it was an old lady from Naples who thought I was texting while taking her order. But she was very old."

We get our exercise, as we climb down the one hundred stairs to our house. Tomorrow will be a long day, but at least the vehicular "wake-up call," with a built-in "snooze" feature—more honking shortly thereafter—ensures that we will get an early start.

Chapter 42

Walk the Path of the Gods, Drive Home with the Devil

Most people flock to the Amalfi Coast to relax on the beaches, eat fantastic food, and stroll down the cobblestone walkways of the picturesque little towns. Instead, I am with David and Colin, trying to figure out where to go, where to park, and where to start our hike on the famous "Path of the Gods." Esther, perhaps wisely, decided to stay at the house to enjoy the relative "peace and quiet" with us gone.

After much trial and error, we figure out where we are and where we want to go. We will walk along the path to Positano and back. Based on our fitness level, we should be able to do it in six hours.

Caves and terraces drop from the cliffs to the sea. The determination and exertion of the people are palpable, as we pass hundreds of dry stone walls, lemon groves, and old vineyards stolen by the mountain. These individuals had colonized the most impractical place on the Amalfi Coast. We walk by homes with farmed terraces, vegetable gardens, and flowers, with no roads leading to them. Far below, waves crash against giant rocks, and an endless succession of cars, buses, and mopeds speeds along the countless hairpin bends.

Colin is in his glory, as he takes photo after photo. The one hundred pounds of additional photo gear he lugs and occasionally pawns off on David are proving useful. A shepherd walks near the path and listens to Neapolitan music on his iPod. We chat and commend him on his ability to hike these paths, as many of the younger generation have left the land.

Colin risks David's life for "the shot"

"I walk a lot," he says, "but I'm still fat 'cause I like to eat a lot."

Not knowing how to respond, I blurt out, "Imagine if you ate a lot and didn't walk a lot, what you would be like." As soon as the words are halfway out of my mouth, I want to take them back, but he good-naturedly laughs it off.

We miss our turnoff and end up much farther along than we expected. Admittedly, I am not as fit as I'd thought. Our original plan of walking both ways is ridiculous. To validate our idea of taking the bus back, it begins to rain.

Despite the pouring rain, when Colin catches two cats sitting on a *motorino*, he takes dozens of photos.

We arrive in the chic resort town of Positano, looking anything but chic ourselves. Soaking wet, we climb into a small bus shelter built into the rock, then wait for the heavy rain to subside. When it clears, we run into an all-purpose store, obviously in desperate need for the tourist season to begin. I ask for a nearby café, and the proprietors offer to make us coffee. I explain that we also need a bathroom, and they offer us theirs. I'm sure that if I asked for a lawnmower, one would turn up within minutes. They are very kind, so

I purchase wine and a few other items and hope the tourists will start coming soon.

The bus arrives, with one of the few remaining seats right behind the driver. I sit down, grateful after six hours of walking—one way.

The bus pulls out, as a well-dressed elderly gentleman strolls out of a bar. The man almost jumps out of his socks when the driver sweeps past him and blasts the horn to warn of impending doom. We entertain ourselves by imagining that he has a pacemaker and his doctor recommended he take some R&R in southern Italy. The warm Amalfi air will do him good. Poor sap.

Perhaps it is my vision, but we appear to be only inches away from the car driving beside us. Later, the men assure me it was not my vision.

I had purchased wine to go with dinner, but as the bus driver maneuvers like a madman, I vow that from now on, I will only buy wine with a screw cap, for times when quick consumption would come in handy.

We run into a traffic jam, and people get out of their cars. The bus driver takes the opportunity to have a smoke and chats with other drivers. Although I'm grateful that my nerves will get a needed break, I'm no fool; once we get going, he will have to make up for lost time.

On the move again, the bus driver proves nothing short of a multitasking miracle—while engaged in a heated negotiation on his cell phone to sell his moped, "Look I'm telling you it's a great price! I will guarantee those are the original kilometers." He gestures with his other hand, while he steers, changes gears, and honks furiously every few seconds. He takes another call, and, despite his thick Neapolitan accent, I can make out something about the price of fish.

I thank him at our stop and tell him his job is not easy.

"It is the job of a slave," he says, repeating it for emphasis.

Chapter 43

Surprise in the Oven

The Amalfi has a reputation for glamor and sophistication. It attracts travelers in search of fine food, eye-popping scenery, and weather that's nothing short of sublime.

After I spent years dreaming about joining the jet set on the Amalfi Coast, it is finally my reality. I'd brought my chicest clothes, summer resort wear. I'd packed sexy high-heeled sandals, and, okay, one pair of squeaky running shoes.

As the rain continues and the temperature drops, I now wear a dirty black sweater and jeans. The laundry we hung yesterday is still wet. I don't bother curling my hair, because the humidity will render it straight and frizzy in no time. The views are five star, but the rain beats in through the glass doors and gushes onto the floor. We close the shutters, and Esther and I count the plastic floral arrangements, while David and Colin play cards.

Getting hungry, we brave the weather and head to the grocery store. Although tasty buffalo mozzarella comes from this area, it is always just beyond Esther's grasp. The larger supermarket was sold out, and while I wait in line at this small grocery, eyeing the one remaining piece, the customer ahead of me purchases it.

I get some milk, and while I shop for a few other items, Esther hurries to the checkout to pay before we do. She insists and grabs the bottle of wine David is holding, to add it to the other groceries. Esther pays and takes the groceries to the car just as I arrive at the cash register with *our* groceries. Meanwhile, an elderly local man returns to the checkout line and wonders what has become of his groceries. The cashier realizes what has happened and tells the customer, who has a good laugh. At the car, I inspect what locals eat: he has good taste in bread, and I'm relieved there are no embarrassing personal hygiene items. If only *he* had bought the last buffalo mozzarella!

We return to the house, and because the rain has stopped, we open the shutters to enjoy our five-star view.

Our five-star view

I preheat the oven, while I prepare lunch. I place the elderly gentleman's bread in the oven to heat it up. On removing the loaf, I find something long and black in the oven right behind the bread. It resembles a dead squirrel.

I shriek and call the men over. They pull it out—a long black sock, confirming that the last guests also had trouble drying their laundry.

To play it safe for dinner, we return to our favourite restaurant. It possesses two important qualities: it's good and cheap, perhaps like us.

After another spectacular dinner, Esther orders a hot chocolate, as the waiter sighs and rolls his eyes.

"It will take me ten minutes to stir this by hand," he says woefully.

After a long while, he returns with the hot chocolate.

"It's rich and thick," Esther says, "like eating a chocolate bar."

Thus, David orders one.

The waiter looks at him and says, "No."

David, assuming the waiter is joking, chuckles and says, "Yes, I will have one."

With a perfect balance of cheerfulness and obstinacy, the waiter replies, "No. Hot chocolate is not for men." He smiles and walks off, leaving David perplexed.

"Yes, you did order it, and yes, he refused," I say. The dry sarcasm and charm of this waiter make the incident forgivable.

The next few days the sun peeks out, and we resume exploring the charming towns along the Amalfi Coast. Colin takes a total of one thousand pictures, and we are ready to receive our master's degree in patience.

After leaving Amalfi to go home, we visit the Reggia di Caserta. It was the largest palace built in Europe during the eighteenth century. It has twelve hundred rooms, including two dozen state apartments, a massive library, and a theater. Of all of the royal residences inspired by the Palace of Versailles, this one bears the greatest resemblance to the original model. The impressive grounds feature an Italian garden, landscaped with vast fields, flowerbeds, and numerous fountains, adorned with sculptural groupings.

Reggia di Caserta

It is endearing to see many families together, touring the palace. The children seem so happy, and I feel as if I'm in a 1950s film.

"It's wonderful to see children with their families and not on their computers," Esther says. Ironically, soon thereafter she Instagrams all of her friends pictures of the palace.

We return home to find that the vines outside our window have grown a foot, and the poppies are making their yearly appearance. The Chianti is lovely, and now that Colin and his camera will soon be leaving I'm happy to call this beautiful place home. Just as I reflect on this, the bus passes and honks several times, bringing back memories of our week on the Amalfi Coast. I laugh heartily, and Colin, noticing, has me pose for "one last shot."

Chapter 44

Enchanting Journeys

Vern is six feet, ten inches tall. He enters our kitchen and smiles on seeing my counter—seemingly custom-built for him. It is love at first sight. This confirms that high heels are not enough for me to work comfortably in the kitchen, but, rather, stilts are required

Kate, his wife, is also enchanted by our house. In her dreams, she has a place like this. She looks at the ceiling with awe. "It's as if each brick tells a story."

I imagine some poor unfortunate soul stuck up on the roof for months under the scorching sun, no doubt cursing each and every brick as he lays it. I keep this to myself. I don't want to ruin the moment, and instead, in a dreamy voice, I repeat what she has said: "Yes, each brick tells a tale." She believes me.

She is also enamored of the huge Venetian-style chandelier hanging from our high-beamed ceiling, over the dining table. She pictures the countless happy meals enjoyed by families during six hundred years in this house. I smile, knowing, in this case, she is correct.

Next, we lead them to the guest bedroom with the iron canopy bed, which, we discover, though charming, was not made for people six feet, ten inches tall. The men dismantle the iron railings, while I take down the canopy fabric. We add an antique blanket box at the foot of the bed and roll up a comforter on it for Vern's feet. Far less romantic, but far more practical.

"Each brick tells a story"

We feast on rabbit with olives and pine nuts, accompanied by roasted potatoes with fennel, wild asparagus, and a mixed salad, served Italian style at the end of the meal. Dessert consists of a heavenly frozen meringue cake from Fior Fiore, a luxury brand from the local supermarket. That's the joy of living in Italy—the quality of the food is so high, I have no qualms serving store-bought items.

After lunch, everyone takes a *pausa*, and Kate and Vern admit they could easily grow accustomed to this lifestyle.

Kate is looking for a handbag that screams, "I visited Florence, and while there I picked up this purse." And indeed she finds one, albeit in San Gimignano.

The hilly countryside boasts a profusion of roses in bloom at the end of each vine. We get a *gelato*, supposedly the best in the world, in the main piazza. Afterward, we drive to Volterra, to see vast fields of green interspersed with abundant patches of fuchsia flowers.

***

Kate has booked a tour of Florence. Her last visit was with two friends who had a checklist of monuments to pose beside and take a selfie, then they rushed to the next one, with no regard for the story or the history behind anything. And because Kate thinks each "brick tells a story," it is only appropriate she hear that story from an expert. She books a tour with Enchanting Journeys.

In an effort to inject a healthy dose of genuine culture and learning into our lives, she has invited us along, and we gratefully accept, wishing to shed our reputation as Philistines. Thanks to our guests, David and I will finally see more of Italy.

The countryside of Florence

Maria Grazia Bravi, the tour escort (which is a higher designation than mere tour guide), lived in London for several years but returned to Italy to be closer to family. She's a true Italian, for although she loves England, she loves her family more. She has a bubbly personality and an accent with a slight British tinge.

Within minutes, we've learned more about Florence than I have in years. She points out the flood markers that indicate the height of the water level during the devastating flooding of the Arno River, as it raged through the streets of downtown Florence. I learn that no one wanted to live near the river in the past, because it was full of malaria mosquitoes. David also discovers that the "free parking" he found in Florence is for residents only. Although white lines in Arezzo designate free parking, in Florence white lines are only for residents. Without all of this ample "free parking," David will plan far fewer visits to Florence.

She tours us through many quaint alleys and cobblestone streets, describing the history to us and many other details that bring the past to life.

We enter the Uffizi Gallery and slowly climb the magnificent staircase. By the second landing, Kate, breathing hard, says, "I'll be right back, I'm just going to go to the hospital for a minute."

After seeing many famous paintings, Kate is inspired and removes her sweater. "According to the ladies of the Renaissance," she says, "it is perfectly acceptable to have round, pudgy arms and still go sleeveless. Some of us became Renaissance women at forty!"

As Maria Grazia describes interesting facets of the lives of many famous painters, we notice a pattern. "He had a very happy/artistic/interesting, or whatever else one could imagine life." But the ending was always the same: "Then he died young."

As the day goes on, the vastness of the Uffizi becomes apparent. Maria Grazia continues with relentless energy, while the rest of us Philistines lose steam and look forward to lunch. We head to the *ristorante* Finisterrae in Piazza Santa Croce. Among all of the well-heeled Florentines, we see an energetic street sweeper who appears to be on speed, skipping as he sweeps in and around the masses with the vitality of the Tasmanian devil in a Bugs Bunny cartoon.

A gypsy begs in front of an outdoor restaurant. An American hands her fifty cents, and to his surprise, she chucks it to the ground in disdain, while her accomplice tries to grab some food off the plate of the stunned American. A man in uniform comes to the rescue. He hurls obscenities at the gypsies, who brush him off without a care. On closer observation, it is evident he is slightly crazed and has taken this calling upon himself. His uniform is worn in several places, his beard is long and scraggly, and his shoes scruffy.

We arrive at the beautiful square and have a wonderful lunch in the garden, of pizza with fresh tomatoes, buffalo mozzarella, and basil.

After lunch, the endless tour continues, and Maria Grazia points out many fascinating aspects of the Duomo and other historic sites. We stand next to the gold circle in the Piazza della Signoria, and she reminds us that *Bonfire of the Vanities* was more than just an American movie. This is the site where Savanarola, along with three other priests, was hanged and ironically burned for his Bonfire of the Vanites, in which he incinerated books and works of art he deemed indecent.

To the bitter end, ten hours later Maria Grazia maintains a smile and walks erect, while the rest of us are in rough shape. Though barely standing, Kate is happy, because, having finally had a real tour of Florence, she will return to Canada with a wealth of information and a lovely couture handbag.

Chapter 45

"See Naples and Die"

If I cannot be elegant in Italy, then surely I can manage this aboard a cruise ship, where mischievous *bella* Italia is not in charge!

I have my hair colored before we leave, and, miraculously, it turns out exactly the way I wanted. The shocked look on my face, however, leaves the hairdresser concerned. "Is the color okay?"

"It's perfect," I say, adjusting my facial expressions to denote pleasure, rather than shock. This is no easy feat, because I was prepared for any other color or style than the one I chose.

I pack a suitcase full of chic clothes, ready to embark on an adventure seeped in sophistication, albeit with my in-laws.

The high-speed train pulls into Roma Tiburtina station. We decide to stay on a few more minutes until the next stop, Roma Termini, the main terminal. This way, we can avoid an additional transfer to Civitavecchia, the port city where the cruise ship departs.

I sit back in my seat, relaxed, and bounce my correctly colored hair.

As the train pulls out of the station, the loudspeaker announces, "Next stop—Naples."

"Naples? Naples? What the heck is going on?" I yell, panicked.

The lady who collects the tickets looks at me with pity and says, "Yes, the next stop is Naples. This train does not stop at Roma Termini."

My legs are shaking, because all I can think of is the cruise ship leaving the port with two fewer passengers who have paid exorbitant sums and my eighty-year-old in-laws wondering what has become of us. I foolishly beg her to stop the train.

A passenger overhears the commotion and, smiling, reassures me, "They say, 'See Naples and die.'"

All I want to do is kill him, because I doubt this applies to seeing the dilapidated train station of Naples.

The conductor pulls up the schedule and fortuitously notes there is a train leaving Naples for Rome five minutes after we arrive. If we have the determination and physical prowess of Speedy Gonzalez, we might just make it. Her pity ends there, as she endeavors to charge us almost one hundred euros for the inadvertent train journey. Meanwhile, our ever-faithful MasterCard will not cooperate. A more determined person I have never met, as the conductor swipes it for the twentieth time, and the charge won't go through. Finally, she gives up, and we get a free ride. She can't really kick us off the moving train, and the next stop is Naples, where we are getting off anyway. With a big smile, I thank the conductor.

With the high-speed train traveling at 190 miles per hour, we arrive in Naples in a flash. We lug our heavy suitcases, barely making the train headed back to Rome, with no time to see Naples and die.

We find the train conductor, who has already been briefed on our situation. He, too, commiserates, as he endeavors to charge us for the train ride *back* to Rome. Our faithful MasterCard once again refuses to cooperate, and after the conductor unsuccessfully runs it through the machine a dozen times, he eventually gives up. I cannot prevent my wide grin, as he hands me my MasterCard, shrugs his shoulders, but also smiles. Another free ride for us.

We arrive in Rome and run with lightning speed to catch the train to the port city. Sweat rolls down my beet-red face, and my newly styled hair needs styling once again. David is also in bad shape, as we embark on our "relaxing vacation" and jump onto the train.

We arrive at the port city and run like maniacs to catch the bus. The driver senses our hurry and overtakes several slower buses. We reach the ship at 6:27 PM, with the last boarding call being at 6:30 PM. The bonus of being the only morons boarding at this late hour is the lack of lines.

We meet up with my in-laws, Filomena and Joe, together with Giorgio and Maria, who are thrilled to see us—Giorgio especially, because, after all, he has been waiting to eat since six o'clock.

With no time to unpack, we hurry down to dinner, where, due to the slow service, I have plenty of time to imagine myself in wrinkled clothes for the remainder of the trip. The ship sails on into the night, and the next morning we awake in Livorno, Italy. Extensive plans are configured, so that David can take his parents to see Pisa and still return in time for lunch. The sacred Italian lunch never takes second place to sightseeing. In case the taxi is late, Filomena scrounges the buffet, packing them a hearty lunch.

The three of them arrive in Pisa and take a few pictures of themselves pretending to hold up the tower. Despite having eaten just hours ago, they arrange a veritable dining table on a bench in the square. Then, although they've already dined twice before eleven in the morning, they return to the cruise ship for lunch. I join them, and lunch almost goes without a hitch, except that once Giorgio sees the menu, he vehemently disagrees with the chef's choice of pasta—insisting that spaghetti, rather than penne, should accompany the tomato sauce. Perhaps the waiter knows better than to argue with an elderly Italian man about pasta and soon thereafter returns with spaghetti.

The following morning the ship anchors in Cannes, France. After breakfast, the six of us walk along the palm-fringed promenade of the stylish French Riviera and stop to take pictures. This is Maria's chance to pull out the food she has lugged from Abruzzo. A clear indication you are traveling with Italians is when they bring food on a cruise. The signs stating that food must not be taken on or off the ship are no deterrent. The long arm of the law takes second place in matters of possible impending hunger. Maria opens the large paper bag filled with roasted chestnuts. Everyone devours them hungrily. Maria flashes me an all-knowing look. After our snack, we will have just enough time to briefly see Cannes before it's time to return to the cruise ship for lunch.

Each morning after breakfast, food is squirreled away for our pre-lunch snack. Then, no matter where we are touring, we will make a mad rush back to the cruise ship to ensure we have lunch by the hour prescribed by Giorgio, regardless of whether any of us are hungry.

We arrive in Naples—David and I for the second time in a matter of days—and find a taxi to take us to the ruins of Herculaneum. Herculaneum's fate runs parallel to that of Pompeii. Destroyed by an earthquake in 62 AD, the city was then submerged in a fifty-foot-thick sea of mud from the 79 AD eruption of Mount Vesuvius, which essentially fossilized all of the buildings and their inhabitants. Herculaneum harbors a wealth of archaeological finds, from ancient advertisements and stylish mosaics to carbonized furniture and terror-struck skeletons. We look at the historic monuments and then spend equal time picnicking among the ruins.

Aware of the reputation the Neapolitans have for reckless driving, I ask the taxi driver to proceed with caution. Perhaps hoping for a larger tip, on arriving back at the cruise ship he says, "Do you see me sweating? It took all my restraint to drive in the manner you wanted!"

He still drove faster than I would have liked, but at least we made it back to the cruise ship in time for lunch, much to Giorgio's delight.

When the cruise is over, I disembark with two pounds of chestnuts Maria stashed away just for David and me. I'm also carrying five pounds of "souvenirs" on my hips and thighs, as a testament to eating several lunches per day.

Chapter 46

Living *La Dolce Vita*—Anywhere!

Many books have been written on life in Italy. As I read the adventures of those who have taken a sabbatical or given up a lucrative career in North America to "live like a local," I smile, for few of us ex-pats can make this claim.

However, if you really want to "live like a local," I do have some suggestions. If you are older and/or retired, first you need to adopt several children and their children. Then lavish most of your time, energy, and money on them, while sacrificing many items on your wish list. If you see a gorgeous leather handbag, don't buy it, but rather purchase an Italian name brand down jacket that your two-year-old adopted granddaughter will soon grow out of. Set the table for twenty on Sundays. Learn to can and jar just about everything. And do it all tirelessly and with a smile.

If you are younger, you must be willing to be adopted by family—not family by North American standards, but one that will dote on you—and you must be prepared to be very, very close. You will live with them, or, if you get married, above them. To fully please your adopted family, you will need to develop a hearty appetite, feign a disdain for drafts, and visit frequently, at least once a day or more.

If my suggestions do not seem feasible or attractive, then you can also come to have the life you always imagined here: sitting relaxed in quaint cafés, sipping an espresso for hours (though this is impossible, given its size). Enjoy long lunches, followed by heavenly *pausas* that are necessitated by the quantity of wine consumed at lunch. I won't destroy your dreams.

However, my conclusion is that we can live the sweet life wherever we may find ourselves, if we choose to. The problem with us North Americans is that what we do when we move to Italy or France—and then write about—we would never do while living in North America. Take a year off and watch our bank accounts diminish? Perish the thought!

The life we desire is not dependent on a geographical location but rather is about the choices we make. We do not need to move to Italy to make our minds over, because not everyone has the circumstances to do so. We need to adjust our views toward money and appreciate the beauty on our own doorstep; then we can live the sweet life, no matter where we are.

So, if you cannot move to Italy, then take time off and rent something in your local countryside. Cook a lovely meal each day, and savor the pleasures that day brings. Rejoice in the multitude of food choices one has in North America; try cheese from a different country each day.

Sit for hours in a pretty café. Order wine with lunch. Forget about the retirement savings plan. Again, forget about the retirement savings plan.

Take a nap wherever you live. What prevents you? Only an attitude, and while we cannot always change our circumstances, we can change the way we think.

Quirky, yet interesting, local characters abound. Fortunately, there are highly incompetent workers wherever we may live, providing a plethora of stories to be told. Take time to get to know them, and while an Italian chimney sweep may seem far more fascinating than a local one (though, I assure you, he is no better dressed), he, too, has a lifetime of stories to share, if only given the chance. The problem may lie in the fact that few of us ever offer him a hefty glass of wine.

Forget about the retirement savings plan.

Love the fact that you have to learn a president's name only once every four years.

In the end, by staying in North America, you may even end up healthier, because you don't lose years off your life when placing a call to a local phone provider during your sojourn in Italy.

Fully aware that every good book or movie has a love story in it, I don't want to disappoint. I have no tales of love being lost and then found again—

tales of well-dressed, heavenly scented, good-looking Italian scoundrels on the prowl. Though I do admit to having one well-dressed (albeit on rare occasions), heavenly scented, good-looking Italian on the prowl, but he is my husband.

We have found *la dolce vita* here. David has learned to eat slowly. A smile crosses his face with each bite, his dimples clearly visible. He has become Italian, despite all of his initial protests, for if Italians have any vices, be they from the work-obsessed North or the so-called work-shy South, one would be food.

David delights in eating juicy red tomatoes from his own garden, picking figs from our tree, drizzling freshly pressed olive oil onto bread, and enjoying reasonably priced, heavenly buffalo mozzarella. Remembering what buffalo mozzarella costs in Canada may just keep us here.

Meanwhile, I love the warmth of the Tuscan sun, the fields that burst with poppies and later give way to acres of brilliant yellow sunflowers, the kindness of friends and neighbors we meet. And of course, the excellent, yet ridiculously cheap, wine.

Poppies in our field

Truly, there is something utterly charming about someone so happy. And as anyone married can attest, when one person is happy, the other one is, too.

We can all benefit from becoming a little bit Italian, to imitate the Italians' focus on spending time every day eating well with family and friends. Despite the difficult economic circumstances some Italians currently find themselves in, they still indulge in the small pleasures of life: a fine espresso, a delectable *gelato*, a pretty pastry. Although I'm not so naïve as to think that all Italians' lives flow as smoothly as their olive oil, I have not met anyone in Italy who is bitterly disappointed with life. If one day we return to Toronto, I am happy knowing that we can also live *la dolce vita* there, for I intend to carry the Italians' easygoing attitude with me. While I'm at it, I will also bring a suitcase or two of their shoes, clothes, and handbags. *Grazie mille,* Italia!

Dear Reader,

Reviews are important to a novel's success and will help other readers find *A Zany Slice of Tuscany*. If you enjoyed my book, please leave a review wherever you purchased it.

I am always delighted to receive email from readers: Ivanka.DiFelice@outlook.com

Happy reading.

Acknowledgments

I want to thank to Patti Waldygo for her superb editing and Joseph Shepherd for his witty cover design.

Grazie mille to my Italian prince, David, who never complained when his Italian world was repeatedly turned upside-down as I continued to write, oblivious to approaching mealtimes. Seems like Nora Ephron got it right when she said, "Secret to life, marry an Italian."

I am grateful to Colin Cummings for teaching me patience, during the hours of my life that passed as I waited for him to get "the shot." Having seen the results, I realize it was worth it. I thank him for the use of his photos (the better ones in the book are his).

A special thanks to my mother, Anica, for her love of books and the humorous stories she wrote throughout the years and for encouraging me to do the same.

My deepest appreciation goes to Filomena Becker and Luca Conficconi who gave me their invaluable input and enthusiasm. Whether it was sincere or not, it greatly inspired me.

And, of course, to Vesna, Tata and to my in-laws, for providing countless inspiration for my stories.

Last but not least, thanks to our two hens, Barbara and Roberta, who ended up being the gift that keeps on giving!